WALKING
AMSTERDAM

WALKING
AMSTERDAM
THE BEST OF THE CITY

Pip Farquharson

NATIONAL GEOGRAPHIC
Washington, D.C.

WALKING AMSTERDAM

CONTENTS

6 INTRODUCTION
8 VISITING AMSTERDAM
10 USING THIS GUIDE

PART **1**

PAGE 12
WHIRLWIND TOURS

14 AMSTERDAM IN A DAY
18 AMSTERDAM IN A WEEKEND
24 AMSTERDAM FOR SHOPPERS
28 AMSTERDAM FOR HISTORY LOVERS
32 AMSTERDAM IN A WEEKEND WITH KIDS

PART **2**

PAGE 40
AMSTERDAM'S NEIGHBORHOODS

44 NIEUWE ZIJDE
64 OUDE ZIJDE
84 JODENBUURT, PLANTAGE, & OOSTERDOK
106 NORTHERN CANALS
128 SOUTHERN CANALS
146 MUSEUM DISTRICT & DE PIJP

PART **3**

PAGE 172
TRAVEL ESSENTIALS

174 TRAVEL ESSENTIALS
180 HOTELS

186 INDEX
191 CREDITS

Previous pages: Crossing Keizersgracht; left: Prinsengracht; right: Montel- baanstoren; above right: the Spiegelkwartier; bottom right: at the Van Gogh Museum

Introduction

I return to Amsterdam two, three, sometimes four times a year. Why? I could pretend it's the Dutch master paintings hanging in the halls of the Rijksmuseum, or the canalside cafés, or the quirky one-theme boutiques (just toothbrushes!). But the real reason is both more complex and much simpler: I come back for the beauty of the place. And I don't need much more of a reminder than the walk I always take along the western arc of concentric canals. This is what I see: the red brick of the cobbled streets and canal houses; the soft curve of the humpbacked bridges, their underbellies strung with lights at night; the straight-backed Amsterdammers sailing by on their bikes. Up above, the rooftops break loose with an exuberant show of stone sculptures: sea monsters, mermaids, saints, and dimpled cherubs. Below me, the gabled world is reflected back, a submerged echo, in the canals they rose out of. The little miracle of the canal belt is one of Europe's largest historic centers, and walking through it is like passing into an ethereal time-warped bubble. If it's a sunny Saturday, I will pass through the Noordermarkt, where vendors roll out wheels of creamy Edam cheese. Or I'll run through the Van Gogh Museum, where the artist's raw Dutch landscapes are capped by an immense, sulky sky. But before dusk I always return to the canals and watch the sun puddle behind those stony mermaids who look ready to dive back into the water. This guide will help you navigate all of Amsterdam's canals and the sublime city they embrace, and intersect, like liquid seams.

Large windows on this building in Westelijk Eilanden in the Northern Canals area are reminders of its former role as a warehouse.

Raphael Kadushin
Award-winning journalist and National Geographic Traveler *magazine writer*

Visiting Amsterdam

Attracting more than 15 million tourists a year, Amsterdam ranks as one of Europe's most popular travel destinations. Visitors come as much for the city's legendary laid-back charm as for its outstanding cultural attractions.

Amsterdam in a Nutshell

Flanking the IJ River to the north, and comprising the Nieuwe Zijde (New Side) and the Oude Zijde (Old Side), Amsterdam's medieval core remains the city's center today. It lies at the heart of the Grachtengordel—a 17th-century ring of canals that was built at the height of the Dutch Golden Age, when trade with the Far East brought tremendous wealth and prosperity to the city. Within these waterways—which radiate from the city center—the Jewish quarter and Plantage district lie to the east, while prestigious canalside houses line the streets to the south and west. Just beyond the canal ring, to the southwest, is the Museum District. Well worth at least a day's visit in its own right, each neighborhood offers a diverse range of sites.

Amsterdam Day-by-Day

Open year-round: Amsterdam Museum; Anne Frank House; Artis Royal Zoo; Heineken Experience; Koninklijk Paleis; Madame Tussauds; Museum het Rembrandthuis; Museum Willet-Holthuysen; Rijksmuseum; Stedelijk Museum; Van Gogh Museum.
Closed Jan. 1, King's Day, and/or Dec. 25: Albert Cuypmarkt (open Jan. 1, King's Day); Allard Pierson Museum; EYE (open Jan. 1, Dec. 25); Foam Museum (open Jan. 1, Dec. 25); Hash, Marihuana, & Hemp Museum (open Jan 1, Dec. 25); Hermitage Amsterdam (open Jan. 1); Het Scheepvaartmuseum; Hortus Botanicus (open King's Day); Kattenkabinett; Museum van Loon; NEMO (open Jan. 1, Dec. 25); Nieuwe Kerk (open King's Day); Oude Kerk (open Jan. 1); Our Lord in the Attic (open Jan. 1, Dec. 25); Tropenmuseum; Verzetsmuseum; Woonbootmuseum.
Closed Mon.: Allard Pierson Museum; Het Scheepvaartmuseum; NEMO (except mid-Feb. to mid-Sep., Oct.); Tropenmuseum (except during school vacations and on various holidays); Verzetsmuseum.
Closed Sat.: Oost-Indisch Huis.
Closed Sun.: Albert Cuypmarkt; Jacob Hooy & Co.; Oost-Indisch Huis; Waterloopleinmarkt; Westerkerk; Zuiderkerk.

Amsterdam's streets and canals are awash with orange—the national color—in celebration of King's Day in April. The holiday is held annually on the monarch's birthday.

Navigating Amsterdam

Amsterdam is *the* city to navigate on foot. You can use the efficient tram and Metro networks to get you from one district to another if you prefer, but almost all of the city's major sites are within walking distance of one another. Alternatively, with 250 miles (400 km) of bike paths, Amsterdam also has a large number of bikes for rent. Although relatively straightforward, the city's layout can cause confusion, as many of the canals—with their stone and wooden bridges—look very similar. A decent city map, available from Tourist Information (see pp. 178–179), will help you navigate until you get your bearings.

Enjoying Amsterdam for Less

Purchase an **I amsterdam City Card** on arrival to make the greatest savings. Available for 24, 48, 72, 96, or 120 hours, the card allows unlimited travel on public transportation and free entry to some 70 museums and attractions, and discounts on a number of others. Additional perks include a free canal-boat ride and reductions on music and theater tickets, as well as special deals in a number of bars and restaurants.

Using This Guide

Each tour is plotted on a map and has been planned to take into account opening hours and the ease of getting from one site to the next. Most tours can be done exclusively on foot, although a couple take advantage of the city's public transportation system and/or its waterways.

Whirlwind Tours

Whirlwind Tours are for people who have only a day or weekend to spend in the city and want to be sure that they see the best of the best. Choose your tour based on your time and interests: One Day; Weekend (Day 1 & Day 2); For Shopping; For History; and With Kids (Day 1 & Day 2).

Tips For the Day and Weekend Tours, a Tips spread following the itinerary map provides insider information on detours from the key sites, extra places to see, nearby cafés and restaurants, and ideas for adapting the tours to suit your interests.

Site Descriptions

In the For Shopping, For History, and With Kids tours, key sites spreads following the maps provide descriptions of the sites and practical information for visitors.

Neighborhood Tours

The six neighborhood tours each begin with an introduction, followed by an itinerary map highlighting the key sites that make up the tour and detailed key sites descriptions. Each tour is followed by an "in-depth" spread showcasing one major site along the route, a "distinctly" Amsterdam spread providing background information on a quintessential element of that neighborhood, and a "best of" spread that groups sites thematically.

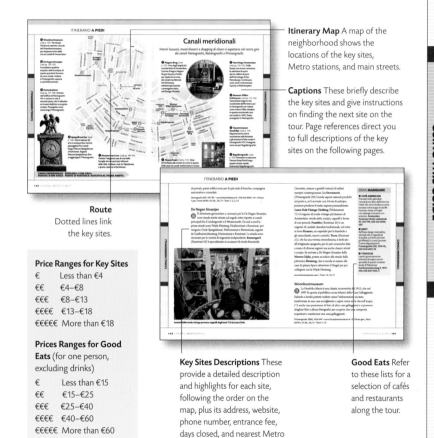

Itinerary Map A map of the neighborhood shows the locations of the key sites, Metro stations, and main streets.

Captions These briefly describe the key sites and give instructions on finding the next site on the tour. Page references direct you to full descriptions of the key sites on the following pages.

USING THIS GUIDE

Route
Dotted lines link the key sites.

Price Ranges for Key Sites

€	Less than €4
€€	€4–€8
€€€	€8–€13
€€€€	€13–€18
€€€€€	More than €18

Prices Ranges for Good Eats (for one person, excluding drinks)

€	Less than €15
€€	€15–€25
€€€	€25–€40
€€€€	€40–€60
€€€€€	More than €60

Key Sites Descriptions These provide a detailed description and highlights for each site, following the order on the map, plus its address, website, phone number, entrance fee, days closed, and nearest Metro station and tram stops.

Good Eats Refer to these lists for a selection of cafés and restaurants along the tour.

PART 1

Whirlwind Tours

WHIRLWIND **TOUR**

7 Red-light District (see pp. 70, 78–79) **This** notorious tourist attraction is best viewed at night, when the neon lights reflect up from the water and the atmosphere on the streets is buzzing.

6 Dam Square (see pp. 50–51) **This is** where it all started. Amsterdam is derived from Amstelredam, the name of the fishing settlement that blocked the Amstel River at the Dam. Head north along Warmoesstraat to the edge of the city's red-light district.

5 Anne Frank House (see pp. 118–121) **The secret** hiding place of the world's most famous diarist. Walk back to the Westermarkt and follow Raadhuisstraat to Dam Square—or hop over the canal ring, taking the more interesting and scenic route.

4 Amsterdam Museum (see pp. 56–59) Follow Amsterdam's fascinating, one-thousand-year journey from a small fishing village to the bustling capital it is today. Walk west onto Prinsengracht and head north.

0   800 meters
0   800 yards

Brouwers-gracht
PALM-GRACHT
LINDEN-GRACHT
Noorderkerk
West-Indisch Huis
HAARLEMMERSTR
WESTERSTRAAT
JORDAAN
EGELANTIERS-GRACHT
Anne Frank House **5**
Westerkerk
Nieuwe Kerk
Dam Square **6**
Beurs van Berlage
Bartolotti Huis
ROZENGRACHT
Koninklijk Paleis
Amsterdam Museum **4**
LAURIER-GRACHT
Woonbootmuseum
De Negen Straatjes
SPUI
Allard Pierson Museum
Bijbels Museum
LEIDSEGRACHT
American Hotel & Café Americain
LEIDSEPLEIN
THORBECKE-PLEIN
Tassenmuseum Hendrikje
Museum van Loon
SPIEGEL-KWARTIER
Amstelkerk
Rijksmuseum **3**
Van Gogh Museum
MUSEUMPLEIN
Stedelijk Museum
MUSEUM QUARTER
H.M.V.RANDWIJK-PLANTSOEN
Singelgracht

AMSTERDAM IN A DAY DISTANCE: 8 MILES (12.5 KM)
TIME: APPROX. 8 HOURS METRO START: CENTRAAL STATION

WHIRLWIND TOURS

Amsterdam in a Day

*Explore this diverse city from every angle
on a packed one-day tour.*

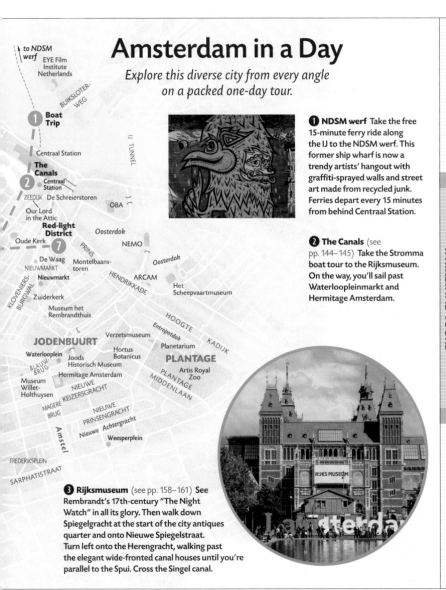

to NDSM werf
EYE Film Institute Netherlands

BUIKSLOTER-WEG

① **Boat Trip**

Centraal Station

The Canals

② Centraal Station

ZEEDIJK De Schreierstoren

IJ TUNNEL

OBA

Our Lord in the Attic

Red-light District

Oude Kerk **⑦**

Oosterdok

PRINS

De Waag Montelbaans-toren

NIEUWMARKT

NEMO

Oosterdok

KLOVENIERSBURGWAL

Nieuwmarkt

HENDRIKKADE ARCAM

Het Scheepvaartmuseum

Zuiderkerk

Museum het Rembrandthuis

HOOGTE

Verzetsmuseum Entrepotdok

KADIJK

JODENBUURT

Hortus Botanicus Planetarium

Waterlooplein Joods Historisch Museum

BLAUWBRUG

Hermitage Amsterdam

NIEUWE KEIZERSGRACHT

PLANTAGE

PLANTAGE MIDDENLAAN

Artis Royal Zoo

Museum Willet-Holthuysen

MAGERE BRUG

NIEUWE PRINSENGRACHT

Nieuwe Achtergracht

Amstel

Weesperplein

FREDERIKSPLEIN

SARPHATISTRAAT

① **NDSM werf** Take the free 15-minute ferry ride along the IJ to the NDSM werf. This former ship wharf is now a trendy artists' hangout with graffiti-sprayed walls and street art made from recycled junk. Ferries depart every 15 minutes from behind Centraal Station.

② **The Canals** (see pp. 144–145) Take the Stromma boat tour to the Rijksmuseum. On the way, you'll sail past Waterlooppleinmarkt and Hermitage Amsterdam.

③ **Rijksmuseum** (see pp. 158–161) **See** Rembrandt's 17th-century "The Night Watch" in all its glory. Then walk down Spiegelgracht at the start of the city antiques quarter and onto Nieuwe Spiegelstraat. Turn left onto the Herengracht, walking past the elegant wide-fronted canal houses until you're parallel to the Spui. Cross the Singel canal.

Tips

This tour combines Amsterdam's very best historic sites with a peek at the city's vibrant and eclectic cultural scene. It is perfect for anyone with only a day to spare.

If time is short, you can customize your tour with these excellent, often less crowded, alternatives and make the most of the suggestions for nearby places to eat.

WHIRLWIND TOURS

❶ **NDSM werf** En route by ferry from ■ **CENTRAAL STATION** (see p. 48) to this former ship wharf, you'll sail past the iconic ■ **EYE** Film Institute Netherlands (see box opposite and p. 39). Resembling a crouching frog, the EYE is part of an inspired regeneration of the former docklands in the north. On arrival at NDSM werf, if you feel like

There are more than 1,700 portraits alone in the Rijksmuseum's collection of paintings.

some breakfast walk to ■ **IJ-KANTINE** (*NDSM-kade 5*), a bright industrial-style café with a waterside terrace; or try ■ **NOORDERLICHT** (*NDSM Plein 102*), within a makeshift greenhouse.

❷ **The Canals** (see pp. 144–145) The best way to see Amsterdam is from the water—especially if you're short of time. The hop-on, hop-off ■ **STROMMA** (*www.stromma.com*) leaves from in front of Centraal Station and will drop you off right outside the Rijksmuseum. On the way, listen to the audio recording pointing out the sites and enjoy the view.

❸ **Rijksmuseum** (see pp. 158–161) After wandering through the museum galleries, head to ■ **MUSEUMPLEIN** (see p. 150). Pick up drinks and snacks from underground supermarket ■ **ALBERT HEIJN** (*Van Baerlestraat 33A*) and enjoy a picnic on its sloping grass rooftop.

Or try ■ COBRA CAFÉ (*Hobbemastraat 18*), dedicated to the mid-20th century CoBrA art movement. Here you can enjoy soups, salads, and sandwiches on Corneille-designed crockery.

❹ **Amsterdam Museum** (see pp. 56–59) Even if you plan to make an in-depth visit to the museum on another day, stop at least to admire the 17th-century paintings at the free-entry ■ AMSTERDAM GALLERY (see p. 57). Or pop, instead, to the adjacent ■ BEGIJNHOF (see pp. 53–54) to see the extraordinary 17th-century Catholic chapel hidden behind the facade of number 30; the 15th-century wooden house at number 34; and Piet Mondrian's altar panels in the English Reformed Church.

❺ **Anne Frank House** (see pp. 118–121) The Jordaan district is a pleasant area for strolling and has several hidden courtyards just waiting to be discovered. The district is also awash with charming canalside cafés and bars. Treat yourself to a typically Dutch dish at ■ THE PANCAKE BAKERY (*Prinsengracht 191*). Alternatively, head to ■ 'T SMALLE (*Egelantiersgracht 12*), where you can relax with a glass of chilled white wine on its peaceful pontoon.

CUSTOMIZING **YOUR DAY**

If you want to visit the EYE, take a free ferry to Buiksloterweg on your return to Centraal Station. If walking around the Rijksmuseum wears you out and you want to skip the Amsterdam Museum, walk to Leidseplein and take tram no. 5 along Marnixstraat, disembarking at Bloemgracht. Walk along this pretty canal to Prinsengracht where you'll find the Anne Frank House; buy your tickets online in advance to avoid long lines.

❻ **Dam Square** (see pp. 50–51) If you still have energy to sightsee, visit the opulent interior of the 17th-century ■ KONINKLIJK PALEIS (see pp. 52–53), originally the town hall. The adjacent 14th-century ■ NIEUWE KERK (see p. 51) now holds exhibitions and is used for royal functions, such as the inauguration of King Willem-Alexander in 2013.

❼ **Red-light District** (see pp. 70, 78–79) Soak up the atmosphere, then enjoy fine Mediterranean dining at ■ BLAUW AAN DE WAL (*Oudezijds Achterburgwal 99*). Its quiet courtyard terrace once belonged to a monastery and is a real find in this otherwise crowded area. Alternatively, head to ■ NIEUWMARKT (see p. 68) to any one of the bars that surround the historic square.

WHIRLWIND TOURS

6 Red-light District (see pp. 70, 78–79)
Sex sells—and nowhere more so than
in Amsterdam's notorious red-lit,
neon-dripping district, which is
almost as old as the city itself.
By all means look, but taking
photos is frowned upon. And
watch out for pickpockets,
particularly if you are
visiting at night!

5 Dam Square (see pp. 50–51) This historic
square is used for rallies, royal weddings, and
other celebrations. Sit on the steps of the
World War II monument admiring the view
of the Koninklijk Paleis and Nieuwe Kerk,
then saunter down Warmoesstraat.

4 Anne Frank House (see pp. 118–121)
See inside the annex where Anne Frank and
her family hid from the Nazis. Head east
across the canals to Dam Square.

3 De Negen Straatjes (see
pp. 138–139) **The Nine Streets**
are crammed with assorted
designer boutiques, vintage
stores, one-of-a-kind shops,
and cute cafés. Spend, spend,
spend, then head north up
Prinsengracht.

Brouwers-gracht
PALM-GRACHT
LIJNBAANSGRACHT
LINDEN-GRACHT
Noorderkerk
Prinsengracht
WESTERSTRAAT
Keizersgracht
JORDAAN
Herengracht
EGELANTIERS-GRACHT
Anne Frank House 4
Westerkerk
ROZENGRACHT
LAURIER-GRACHT
De Negen Straatjes
3
Woonbootmuseum
MARNIXSTRAAT
Bijbels Museum
KONINGS-PLEIN
LEIDSEGRACHT
American Hotel & Café Americain
LEIDSEPLEIN
SPIEGEL-KWARTIER
STADHOUDERSKADE
Lijnbaans-gracht
WETERINGSCHANS
Rijksmuseum
MUSEUMPLEIN

**AMSTERDAM IN A WEEKEND DAY 1 DISTANCE: 3 MILES (5 KM)
TIME: APPROX. 7 HOURS METRO START: NIEUWMARKT**

Amsterdam in a Weekend

Embark on an almost circular tour of Amsterdam's most visited sites, and indulge in some shopping along the way.

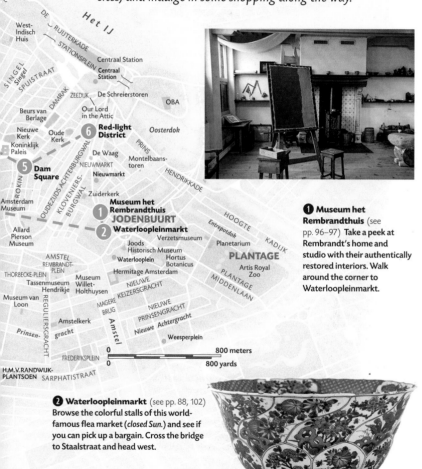

West-Indisch Huis

Het IJ

DE RUIJTERKADE
STATIONSPLEIN
SINGEL
Singel
SPUISTRAAT
DAMRAK
ZEEDIJK
Centraal Station
Centraal Station
De Schreierstoren
OBA

Beurs van Berlage
Our Lord in the Attic
6 Red-light District
Oosterdok
Oosterdok

Nieuwe Kerk
Koninklijk Paleis
Oude Kerk
OUDEZIJDS ACHTERBURGWAL
NIEUWMARKT
De Waag
PRINS
HENDRIKKADE
Montelbaans-toren

5 Dam Square
ROKIN
KLOVENIERSBURGWAL
OUDEZIJDS VOORBURGWAL
Nieuwmarkt
Zuiderkerk

Amsterdam Museum

Allard Pierson Museum

AMSTEL
REMBRANDT-PLEIN
THORBECKE-PLEIN
Tassenmuseum Hendrikje
Museum van Loon
REGULIERSGRACHT
Amstelkerk
Prinsen-gracht
MAGERE BRUG
Amstel

1 Museum het Rembrandthuis
JODENBUURT
2 Waterlooplein markt
Verzetsmuseum
Joods Historisch Museum
Waterlooplein
Hortus Botanicus
Museum Willet-Holthuysen
Hermitage Amsterdam
NIEUWE KEIZERSGRACHT
NIEUWE PRINSENGRACHT
Nieuwe Achtergracht
Weesperplein

HOOGTE
Entrepotdok
Planetarium
KADIJK
PLANTAGE
Artis Royal Zoo
PLANTAGE MIDDENLAAN

FREDERIKSPLEIN
H.M.V. RANDWIJK-PLANTSOEN SARPHATISTRAAT

0 _____ 800 meters
0 _____ 800 yards

1 Museum het Rembrandthuis (see pp. 96–97) Take a peek at Rembrandt's home and studio with their authentically restored interiors. Walk around the corner to Waterloopleinmarkt.

2 Waterloopleinmarkt (see pp. 88, 102) Browse the colorful stalls of this world-famous flea market (*closed Sun.*) and see if you can pick up a bargain. Cross the bridge to Staalstraat and head west.

Amsterdam in a Weekend

Round off a day immersed in culture with cocktails and a relaxed evening cruise along Amsterdam's canals.

❶ Rijksmuseum (see pp. 158–161) **If you only have time for one painting, make sure it's Rembrandt's "The Night Watch." Walk up Stadhouderskade to the entrance of Vondelpark.**

❷ Vondelpark (see pp. 154–155) What Central Park is to New York, Vondelpark is to Amsterdam. Stroll through or have a picnic, then walk up the path to the bridge, and head south along Van Baerlestraat.

❸ Stedelijk Museum (see pp. 150–151) Amsterdam's museum of modern art, contemporary art, and design includes work by Andy Warhol, Gilbert & George, Karel Appel, and Willem de Kooning. After admiring the collection, pop next door to the Van Gogh Museum.

ADMIRAAL DE RUIJTERWEG

Kostverlorenvaart

BELLAMYPLEIN

OUD WEST

KINKERSTRAAT

P. LANGENDIJKSTRAAT

OVERTOOM

Vondelpark
❷

WHIRLWIND TOURS

AMSTERDAM IN A WEEKEND DAY 2 DISTANCE: 2 MILES (3.5 KM) TIME: APPROX. 8 HOURS START: RIJKSMUSEUM

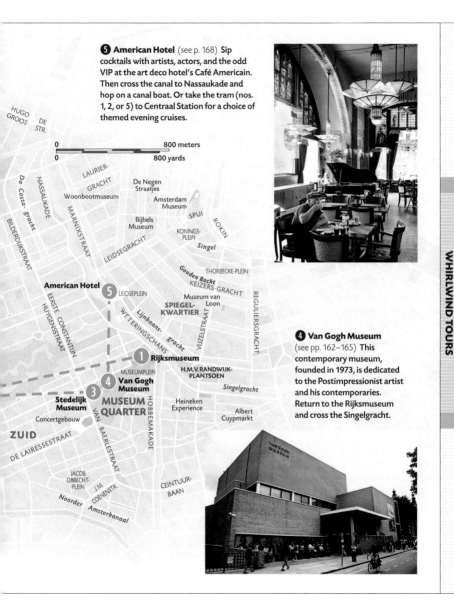

⑤ American Hotel (see p. 168) Sip cocktails with artists, actors, and the odd VIP at the art deco hotel's Café Americain. Then cross the canal to Nassaukade and hop on a canal boat. Or take the tram (nos. 1, 2, or 5) to Centraal Station for a choice of themed evening cruises.

0 ———— 800 meters
0 ———— 800 yards

HUGO GROOT- STR.
DE STR.

Da Costa- gracht

NASSAUKADE

BILDERDIJKSTRAAT

LAURIER- GRACHT

Woonbootmuseum

De Negen Straatjes

MARNIXSTRAAT

Bijbels Museum

Amsterdam Museum

SPUI

KONINGS- PLEIN

Singel

LEIDSEGRACHT

ROKIN

Gouden Bocht

THORBECKE-PLEIN

KEIZERSGRACHT

American Hotel

⑤ LEIDSEPLEIN

EERSTE CONSTANTIJN HUYGENSSTRAAT

WETERINGSCHANS

Lijnbaans- gracht

SPIEGEL- KWARTIER

VIJZELSTRAAT

Museum van Loon

REGULIERSGRACHT

① Rijksmuseum

MUSEUMPLEIN

H.M.V. RANDWIJK- PLANTSOEN

Singelgracht

④ Van Gogh
② ④ **Museum**

Stedelijk Museum

③ **MUSEUM QUARTER**

VAN BAERLESTRAAT

HOBBEMAKADE

Heineken Experience

Albert Cuypmarkt

Concertgebouw

ZUID

DE LAIRESSESTRAAT

JACOB OBRECHT- PLEIN

J.M. COENENSTR.

CEINTUUR- BAAN

Noorder Amsterkanaal

④ Van Gogh Museum (see pp. 162–165) This contemporary museum, founded in 1973, is dedicated to the Postimpressionist artist and his contemporaries. Return to the Rijksmuseum and cross the Singelgracht.

Tips

Two days in Amsterdam afford enough time to get a true sense of this city's rich history and its tremendous cultural diversity. Here you'll find information on detours to nearby sites and local cafés and restaurants, as well as suggestions for customizing the tour to suit your own interests.

DAY 1

❷ **Waterloopleinmarkt** (see pp. 88, 102) Next door to the market is ■ **DUTCH NATIONAL OPERA & BALLET** (see pp. 82–83), which has an excellent program of ballet and opera, interspersed with performances from international dance companies. ■ **PUCCINI** (*Staalstraat 21*) is a perfect pit stop to enjoy Italian soup and salads.

CUSTOMIZING **YOUR DAY**

Amsterdam has an extraordinary year-round cultural scene. If you only have one night in Amsterdam, why not check out what's on offer? On the I Amsterdam website (www.iamsterdam.com) you can find a guide dedicated to each day's various musical events and festivals and instructions for purchasing your ticket. There really is something for everyone, from a night at the most popular clubs to a series of family friendly events.

Or walk a few doors to their store, ■ **PUCCINI BOMBONI** (*Staalstraat 17*), and buy some tea- or pepper-flavored chocolate. Don't leave the street without a visit to ■ **DROOG** (see p. 166), purveyors of top-notch Dutch design—with a twist.

❸ **De Negen Straatjes** (see pp. 138–139) This is a great area to take a walk and enjoy the display windows of an array of unique shops that sell a variety of products, including specialty foods. For example, offering more than 200 different types of cheese, ■ **DE KAASKAMER** (see p. 126) couldn't be a better place for edible souvenirs.

❹ **Anne Frank House** (see pp. 118–121) The nearby ■ **WESTERKERK** (see p. 111), dating from 1620, is where Rembrandt is buried in a pauper's grave. From April to October, you can climb its tower. Look on the south side for a statue of Anne Frank by Dutch sculptor Mari Andriessen, renowned for his work memorializing victims of the holocaust. Another memorial to the persecuted—this time gays and lesbians—is the ■ HOMOMONUMENT (see pp. 110–111). Pop into the ■ PINK POINT kiosk *(corner of Raadhuisstraat/ Keizersgracht)* for postcards and souvenirs such as T-shirts.

DAY 2

❶ **Rijksmuseum** (see pp. 158–161) If you feel like a refreshing dip mid-tour, ■ ZUIDERBAD (see pp. 39, 168) is a gorgeous art nouveau swimming pool dating from 1911. Alternatively, catch a daytime concert of classical music at the ■ CONCERTGEBOUW (see pp. 83, 151–153); it's world-renowned for its acoustics.

❷ **Vondelpark** (see pp. 154–155) One of Amsterdam's best-kept secrets can be found in the middle of the park: The ■ BLAUWE THEEHUIS *(www.blauwethee huis.nl)* resembles a flying saucer. Sit on its upper level and you'll feel as if you're at one with the trees. Next door is an ■ OPEN-AIR THEATER *(www.openlucht theater.nl)*, which stages all manner of productions in the summer. For a more unusual pit stop, head to ■ HOLLANDSCHE MANEGE (see p. 38), riding stables with a

The Westerkerk from Prinsengracht

café overlooking the sandy arena where classes take place. Before you leave the park, see if you can find the now rather shabby sculpture by Picasso—he donated it to the city in 1965—and keep an eye out for the park's wild parakeets.

❺ **American Hotel** (see p. 168) Within spitting distance of the hotel are ■ MELKWEG (see p. 83) and ■ PARADISO (see p. 27). For fast, fresh noodles, head to ■ WAGAMAMA *(Max Euweplein 10)*. You can pick up the hop-on, hop-off ■ STROMMA *(www.stromma.com)* from the pontoon opposite the American Hotel but check times beforehand: Depending on the time of year, they might not run in the evening. If you want a specific canal cruise—one with Dutch cheese and wine, pizza, or dinner—head to ■ CENTRAAL STATION (see p. 48).

Amsterdam for Shoppers

From diamonds and handbags to the latest haute couture, this "shop until you drop" day in Amsterdam ends with food, fun, and music.

0   800 meters
0   800 yards

6 Paradiso (see p. 27) Catch a late-night show at the Paradiso, one of Amsterdam's premier live-music venues. Established in a former church during the 1960s, and complete with its original stained glass, the club is endearingly known as the Pop Temple.

5 P. C. Hooftstraat (see pp. 27, 153–154) Step ashore at Hooftstraat, Amsterdam's equivalent of Rodeo Drive. The street is spangled with high-class stores, such as Gucci and Cartier, plus a handful of Dutch designer brands. Around dusk, take the tram (no. 3 or 19) to De Clercqstraat and walk east to Rozengracht.

4 Royal Afternoon Tea at Amstel Hotel (see p. 27) A spot of tea and a plate of cracknel—and perhaps even a sip of champagne—are the order of the day in the elegant Amstel Lounge, where Dutch high society has been consorting since the 1860s. Then, head down the Singelgracht.

AMSTERDAM FOR SHOPPERS DISTANCE: 5.7 MILES (9.2 KM)
TIME: APPROX. 8.5 HOURS METRO START: NIEUWMARKT

Map labels: ROZENGRACHT · LAURIER-GRACHT · KEIZERS-GRACHT · HEREN-GRACHT · Woonbootmuseum · De Negen Straatjes 2 · MARNIXSTRAAT · Bijbels Museum · LEIDSEGRACHT · LEIDSEPLEIN · SPIEGEL-KWARTIER · Paradiso 6 · Lijnbaansgracht · P. C. Hooftstraat 5 · P. C. HOOFTSTRAAT · Rijksmuseum · Stedelijk Museum · Van Gogh Museum · MUSEUMPLEIN

WHIRLWIND TOURS

1 Gassan Diamonds (see p. 26) Diamonds are not the only things that glitter at Gassan. The cutting and polishing take place inside the Boas Building, one of Amsterdam's 19th-century architectural gems. After the free factory tour, head on foot to Waterlooplein, where you can cross the Amstel River. Follow the Amstel west, to the Singel canal, and hang a left onto Huidenstraat.

2 De Negen Straatjes (see pp. 26, 138–139) Enter any one of the nine streets that comprise this upscale retail area in the heart of the Southern Canals district. Pick your way through more than 40 boutiques, finishing up on Herengracht. Turn right, and walk back toward the Amstel River.

3 Utrechtsestraat (see p. 26) This street, which crosses a number of canals, is full of trendy concept stores, high-fashion boutiques, and designer furniture shops, as well as being home to Concerto, a music shop for old-style music buffs and hip young vinyl lovers.

Gassan Diamonds

1 Diamonds are everyone's best friend at Gassan, Amsterdam's paramount "rock" factory and dealer. Watch skilled craftsmen cut and polish diamonds during the free tour, and then check out the factory boutique, where you'll find simple, unset stones, stunning necklaces, or even a gem-studded pocket watch. The factory building is equally dazzling. One of few plants still operating in the city center, this neoclassical masterpiece was erected in 1899.

Nieuwe Uilenburgerstraat 173–175, 1011 LN • www.gassan.com • 020 622 533 • Metro: Nieuwmarkt or Waterlooplein • Tram: 14

De Negen Straatjes

2 Wedged between the Singel canal and Prinsengracht, on the western side of the old town, the Nine Streets is one of the city's most intriguing retail zones. Housed in 17th-century canal houses, many of the shops are one-off or quirky, with an eclectic selection that ranges from artisanal soaps and handcrafted jewelry to vintage clothing and designer frocks.

Tram: 2, 11, 12, 13, 17

Bags by Chanel, Hermès, and Louis Vuitton feature at the Tassenmuseum Hendrikje.

Utrechtsestraat

3 This city center street extends from Frederiksplein north to Rembrandtplein. It's home to family-run specialty shops where you can find original clothing and objects, often produced by artisans that have worked in their field for generations. Obviously, there are a number of outposts of more famous brand names, as well. This could be the place to find a memento that's more than a simple souvenir.

Tram: 4

Royal Afternoon Tea at Amstel Hotel

4 Whether you're partial to jasmine, oolong, or Darjeeling golden flowery orange pekoe, afternoon tea in the **Amstel Lounge** is an affair to remember. Grab a table with a view over the river, order your favorite tea, and dig into Dutch treats, such as cracknel biscuits and *hazelino* pastries.

Professor Tulpplein 1, 1018 GX • www.amsterdam.
intercontinental.com • 020 622 6060 • €€€€ • Metro:
Weesperplein • Tram: 1, 7, 19

P. C. Hooftstraat

5 Located in the posh Oud-Zuid (Old South) neighborhood, P. C. Hooftstraat is Amsterdam's fashion central, its 19th-century town houses filled with luxury boutiques both domestic and foreign. International names to look out for include Chanel, Gucci, Hermès, and Louis Vuitton. Those looking for Dutch brands will find Claudia Sträter and Oger. From outdoor fashion shows to its celebrated stiletto race, the street also hosts fashion-related special events throughout the year.

Jacob van Lennepkade 334H • www.pchooftstraat.nl • Tram: 7, 17

Paradiso

6 Along with the Concertgebouw (see p. 83), this is Amsterdam's premier live-music venue. Lodged in a dark and brooding 19th-century church, this pop temple has been hosting rock and pop legends since the late 1960s, when it started life as a hippie squat. There are usually two live-music shows per night, including a midnight special.

Weteringschans 6, 1017 SG • www.paradiso.nl • 020 626 4521 • €€–€€€ • Metro:
Vijzelgracht • Tram: 2, 11, 12

GOOD **EATS**

■ **CAFÉ AMERICAIN**
A feast for the eyes and palate, this popular café in the Amsterdam American Hotel is known for its original art nouveau décor and excellent seafood. **Leidsekade 97, 1017 PN, 020 556 3000, €€–€€€€**

■ **THE PANTRY**
Cozy up in this café dedicated to traditional dishes like salted pork and *zuurkoolstamppot* (mashed potatoes with sauerkraut). **Leidsekruisstraat 21, 1017 RE, 020 620 0922, €–€€**

■ **PURI MAS**
Rijsttafel (rice table) and other Indonesian meals are the forte of this East Indian eatery. The menu is sprinkled with gluten-free, halal, and vegetarian dishes. **Lange Leidsedwarsstraat 37–41, 1017 NG, 020 627 7627, €–€€€**

Amsterdam for History Lovers

*From medieval times to World War II, the Dutch
metropolis offers rich and varied treasures for history buffs.*

❶ Amsterdam Museum (see pp. 30, 56–59)
Take a trip back in time at this excellent history museum, and witness the city's rise from fishing village to global powerhouse. Walk north along Nieuwezijds Voorburgwal and turn right onto Paleisstraat and Dam Square.

❷ Dam Square (see pp. 30, 50–51)
Visit the 17th-century Koninklijk Paleis, 15th-century Nieuwe Kerk, and other historic buildings flanking one of Europe's oldest and best public squares. Exit the square down wide Damrak and turn left onto narrow Haringpakkerssteeg.

❸ West-Indisch Huis (see p. 30)
Admire the edifice of this building, from which Holland controlled New Amsterdam (now New York) and the rest of its American empire. Backtrack to Damrak and follow busy Prins Hendrikkade past the baroque Sint Nicolaaskerk.

❹ De Schreierstoren (see pp. 30, 72)
Serving as a café today, this tower is one of the few remaining structures that made up the city's original medieval walls. Hang a right onto Geldersekade and head for Nieuwmarkt.

❺ De Waag (see pp. 31, 68–69)
The city's oldest remaining secular structure has served as a city gate, guildhall, and fire station during its 500 years of existence. The technology-driven Waag Society hosts events and interactive exhibitions on the second floor. You'll find a café on the first floor.

**AMSTERDAM FOR HISTORY LOVERS DISTANCE: 2.8 MILES (4.5 KM)
TIME: APPROX. 8 HOURS TRAM START: SPUI**

WHIRLWIND TOURS

6 Oost-Indisch Huis (see p. 31) This stout, brick building was headquarters of the world's first multinational corporation, the powerful Dutch East India Company (VOC). Part of the University of Amsterdam, the meticulously restored complex features an impressive inner courtyard and period artworks. Head southeast on Oude Hoogstraat and Nieuwe Hoogstraat. Turn right onto Sint Antoniesbreestraat and continue on Jodenbreestraat.

Westelijke Eilanden
Bickers-eiland

HAARLEMMER-BUURT

WESTER DOKSDIJK

Het IJ

DE RUIJTERKADE

STATIONSPLEIN

0 — 800 meters
0 — 800 yards

HAARLEMMERSTR

West-Indisch Huis 3

Stationsplein

Centraal Station
Centraal Station

SPUISTRAAT

SINGEL

Herengracht
Singel gracht

DAMRAK

WARMOESSTRAAT

ZEEDIJK

4 De Schreierstoren

RED-LIGHT DISTRICT

Beurs van Berlage
Nieuwe Kerk
Oude Kerk

Oosterdok

Dam Square

RAADHUIS STRAAT

Koninklijk Paleis

ROKIN

OUDEZIJDS VOORBURGWAL

PRINS

5 De Waag

Montelbaans-toren

NIEUWMARKT
Nieuwmarkt

HENDRIKKADE

SPUISTR.

6 Oost-Indisch Huis

Zuiderdok

1 Amsterdam Museum

Allard Pierson Museum

SPUI

KONINGS-PLEIN

Singel

ROKIN

Amstel

JODENBUURT

Waterlooplein

AMSTEL REMBRANDT-PLEIN

BLAUW-BRUG

THORBECKE-PLEIN

Gouden Bocht
KEIZERS-GRACHT

SPIEGEL-KWARTIER

VIJZELSTRAAT

Museum van Loon
Prinsen-gracht

REGULIERSGRACHT

Amstelkerk

gracht

Amstel

MAGERE BRUG

Museum het Rembrandthuis 7

Joods Historisch Museum
Museum Willet-Holthuysen

NIEUWE KEIZERSGRACHT

NIEUWE PRINSENGRACHT

Nieuwe Achtergracht

Weesperplein

Hortus Botanicus

Verzetsmuseum 8

HOOGTE

Entrepotdok

KADIJK

Planetarium

PLANTAGE

Artis Royal Zoo

PLANTAGE MIDDENLAAN

SARPHATISTRAAT

7 Museum het Rembrandthuis (see pp. 31, 96–97) For nearly 20 years, the Dutch master lived and painted in this three-story house, which now contains more than 300 of his works. On leaving, turn right and follow Jodenbreestraat and its continuations to Plantage Kerklaan.

8 Verzetsmuseum (see pp. 31, 92–93) Fast-forward to the 20th-century in a museum dedicated to World War II and the Dutch Resistance against brutal Nazi Occupation.

Amsterdam Museum

1 The city's history museum examines Amsterdam's rich past through a microscope of hands-on exhibits, digital displays, short films, and hundreds of original artifacts.

Kalverstraat 92, 1012 PH | Sint Luciënsteeg 27, 1012 PM • www.amsterdammuseum.nl • 020 523 1822 • €€ • Metro: Rokin • Tram: 2, 4, 11, 12, 14, 24

Dam Square

2 The heart of Amsterdam for nearly 800 years, Dam Square is a swirl of traffic, pedestrians, and architecture from several ages. The city's town hall (later the Koninklijk Paleis) epitomizes Dutch wealth and prestige at the height of the Golden Age. Built using stone imported from Germany, no expense was spared either in its construction or in its lavish marble interiors. Pop into the Nieuwe Kerk opposite, for a glimpse of its spectacular 17th-century organ.

Metro: Centraal Station • Tram: 2, 4, 11, 12, 13, 14, 17

Dutch architect J. J. P. Oud designed the National Monument that stands in Dam Square, in 1956.

West-Indisch Huis

3 The Dutch West India Company managed trade in the Americas from here. Slip into the building's courtyard off Herenmarkt to see a statue of **Peter Stuyvesant,** the governor of 17th-century New Amsterdam (New York).

Herenmarkt 97, 1013 EC • www.john-adams.nl • 020 624 7280 • Tram: 1, 2, 5, 13, 17 • Bus: 18, 21

De Schreierstoren

4 Admire the acutely pitched roof of this 15th-century tower. It fronts the docks from which Henry Hudson first set sail for North America.

Prins Hendrikkade 94, 1012 AE • Metro: Centraal Station or Nieuwmarkt • Tram: 2, 4, 11, 12, 13, 14, 17

De Waag

5 Erected as a city gate in 1456, De Waag takes it name from its later (ca 1600) function as a weigh house for local traders. See if you can identify the guild emblems—blacksmith, painter, surgeon, mason—above the various entrances, dating from when it served as a guildhall.

Nieuwmarkt 4, 1012 CR • Metro: Nieuwmarkt • Tram: 4, 14

Oost-Indisch Huis

6 Decorative scrollwork and sandstone details decorate the headquarters of the former Dutch East India Company, which controlled trade with Asia, including the lucrative spice trade.

Oude Hoogstraat 24, 1012 CE • Closed Sat., Sun. • Metro: Nieuwmarkt • Tram: 4, 14

Museum het Rembrandthuis

7 Commune with the spirit of the Dutch master as you tour rooms arranged almost exactly as they were when he lived here.

Jodenbreestraat 4, 1011 NK • www.rembrandthuis.nl • 020 520 0400 • €€ • Closed King's Day and Dec. 25 • Metro: Nieuwmarkt or Waterlooplein • Tram: 14

Verzetsmuseum

8 Dutch Resistance against Nazi Occupation is the focus of this somber, yet captivating collection in the Plantage district. Among the exhibits are a hollow chessboard used for hiding papers and rudimentary tools used for forging identity cards.

Plantage Kerklaan 61, 1018 CX • www.verzetsmuseum.org • 020 620 2535 • €€ • Closed Jan. 1, King's Day, and Dec. 25 • Metro: Waterlooplein • Tram: 14

GOOD **EATS**

■ **BRASSERIE-DE-POORT**
At one of Amsterdam's oldest and most venerable restaurants house specialties include steak and pea soup. **Nieuwezijds Voorburgwal 176–180, 1012 SJ, 020 714 2000, €€**

■ **D'VIJFF VLIEGHEN**
Spread across five canal houses, this restaurant serves traditional Dutch cuisine among Rembrandt etchings. **Spuistraat 294–302, 1012 VX, 020 530 4060, €€€**

■ **PLANCIUS**
Good-value lunches and bistro dinners are available next door to the Verzetsmuseum. **Plantage Kerklaan 61, 1018 CX, 020 330 9469, €€**

■ **VOC-CAFÉ**
Treat yourself to a *Schoot-An jenever* (VOC-style gin) in this atmospheric café with views across the Geldersekade. **Prins Hendrikkade 94, 1012 AE, 020 428 8291, €€**

Amsterdam in a Weekend with Kids

From a rooftop viewpoint to historic gardens with a centuries-old tree, day one of your family weekend reveals an incredibly diverse city.

❺ Hortus Botanicus (see pp. 35, 90–91) **Take a leisurely stroll through Amsterdam's long-established botanical garden—one of the oldest in Europe—where butterflies flutter freely in the Butterfly Greenhouse. What better way to recharge your batteries at the end of a fun-filled day?**

❹ Tropenmuseum (see pp. 35, 170–171) **Explore this extensive collection of artifacts from the tropics. The museum's award-winning junior section features shows, activities, and exhibits for kids. Take the tram (no. 14) to Plantage Kerklaan.**

Centraal Station
Centraal Station

SINGEL SPUISTRAAT
Singel
ZEEDIJK
Beurs van Berlage DAMRAK
WARMOESSTRAAT
Nieuwe Kerk
Oude Kerk
Koninklijk Paleis DAM OUDEZIJDS VOORBURGWAL De Waag
ROKIN NIEUWMARKT
SPUISTR. Nieuwmarkt
Amsterdam Museum
Zuiderkerk
Museum het Rembrandthuis
SPUI
ROKIN
KONINGS-PLEIN
Amstel
Singel AMSTEL
REMBRANDT-PLEIN
THORBECKE-PLEIN
Tassenmuseum
Hendrikje Museum Willet-Holthuysen
KEIZERS-GRACHT
REGULIERSGRACHT
Amstelkerk
Prinsen- gracht
FREDERIKSPLEIN
SARPHATISTRAAT
Singelgracht

**WEEKEND WITH KIDS DAY 1 DISTANCE: 4.5 MILES (7.2 KM)
TIME: APPROX. 7 HOURS METRO START: CENTRAAL STATION**

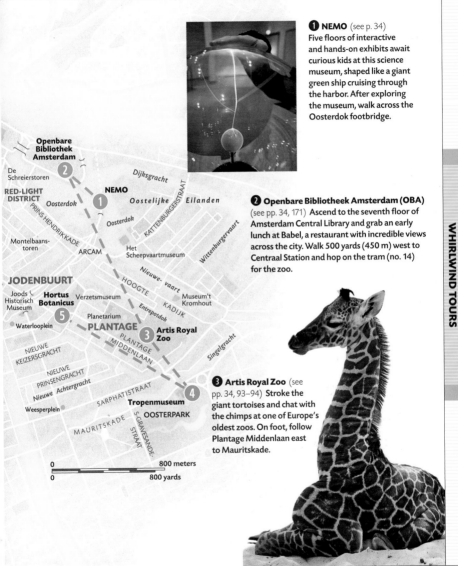

❶ NEMO (see p. 34)
Five floors of interactive and hands-on exhibits await curious kids at this science museum, shaped like a giant green ship cruising through the harbor. After exploring the museum, walk across the Oosterdok footbridge.

❷ Openbare Bibliotheek Amsterdam (OBA)
(see pp. 34, 171) Ascend to the seventh floor of Amsterdam Central Library and grab an early lunch at Babel, a restaurant with incredible views across the city. Walk 500 yards (450 m) west to Centraal Station and hop on the tram (no. 14) for the zoo.

❸ Artis Royal Zoo (see pp. 34, 93–94) Stroke the giant tortoises and chat with the chimps at one of Europe's oldest zoos. On foot, follow Plantage Middenlaan east to Mauritskade.

NEMO

1 Bubbles, balls, and dominoes help kids learn about science inside this creative technology museum designed by Renzo Piano. Among its many highlights are a Rube Goldberg-like chain-reaction circuit, an entire floor dedicated to how we humans work, and a huge science laboratory where kids can experiment to their hearts' content, dressed up in white lab coats and protective goggles.

Oosterdok 2, 1011 VX • www.nemosciencemuseum.nl • 020 531 3233 • €€ • Closed Mon. (except from mid-Feb. to mid-Sep. and Oct.), King's Day • Metro: Centraal Station

Openbare Bibliotheek Amsterdam

2 One of Europe's largest public libraries has much more to offer than books. Amsterdam Central Library is a stunning example of modern public architecture and a great place to snatch a bird's-eye view of the harbor and old town from the rooftop café and terrace.

Oosterdokskade 143, 1011 DL • www.oba.nl • 020 523 0900 • Metro: Centraal Station • Tram: 2, 4, 12, 14, 26

Artis Royal Zoo

3 More than 900 species dwell inside this leafy precinct in central Amsterdam. The collection is especially strong on rare wildlife, such as the African wild dog and Madagascar lemur. Founded in 1838, the zoo has many historic buildings (which were recently restored) and there are always new attractions, such as the sprawling African plains enclosure, the butterfly house, and the Insectarium. To get the most from your visit check its program of daily events. You might be in time to catch the lions, penguins, or macaques at feeding time, or to join a training session with the sea lions.

Plantage Kerklaan 38–40, 1018 CZ • www.artis.nl • 020 5233 670 • €€€ • Metro: Waterlooplein • Tram: 14

SAVVY **TRAVELER**

If it's raining, skip Hortus Botanicus and head to **TunFun Speelpark** *(Meester Visserplein 7, 1011 RD)*. Tucked beneath Visserplein square, this underground playground offers giant slides, ball courts, and rope bridges. Admission price for adults is reduced and the ticket includes a cup of coffee or tea.

Tropenmuseum

④ Part of the Royal Tropical Institute, this innovative ethnographic museum has abandoned the usual geographical layout and examines the cultures of the world through universal themes and current social issues. Tropenmuseum Junior is geared specifically toward kids. There are plenty of things to occupy Mom and Dad too. You can also take a guided tour of the building that houses the museum and discover its fascinating history, but it's rather expensive.

Children delight in wood carvings from New Guinea at the Tropenmuseum.

Linnaeusstraat 2, 1092 CK • www.tropenmuseum.com • 020 568 8200 • €€ • Closed most Mon. (except during school vacations and on various holidays), Jan. 1, King's Day, and Dec. 25 • Tram: 3, 7, 14, 19

Hortus Botanicus

⑤ The world's largest and smallest seeds, the fattest and shortest trees, and a water lily almost as big as a boat are among the discoveries that kids can make among the 4,000 plant species at Amsterdam's botanical garden. A Superplants map, available in English, leads children to 15 of the gardens' record-making plants. Children are also encouraged to learn about endangered species, using a booklet on biodiversity (also in English), which can be bought from the ticket office, and which discusses 15 threatened plants in the garden. Recent additions to the site are a photosynthesis exhibition and a greenhouse dedicated to cacti and other desert plants. And be sure not to miss the 300-year-old Eastern cycad from South Africa.

Plantage Middenlaan 2A, 1018 DD • www.dehortus.nl • 020 625 9021 • € • Closed Jan. 1 and Dec. 25 • Metro: Waterlooplein • Tram: 14

Amsterdam in a Weekend with Kids

Canal boats are your means of getting around on day two, an outing that includes movies, museums, and a magical indoor pool.

❶ Canal Boat Trip (see p. 38) Purchase a one-day Stromma ticket at the kiosk outside Centraal Station and get on board. The route takes you down the Prinsengracht. Disembark at Leidseplein quay and walk west on Vondelstraat.

❷ Hollandsche Manege (see p. 38) Holland's version of the Spanish Riding School is housed in an elegant indoor riding facility. After, retrace your steps one block and turn right into the park.

Map labels: JORDAAN, NASSAUKADE, Singelgracht, EGELANTIERS-GRACHT, Anne Frank House, Westerkerk, ROZENGRACHT, Pulitzer Hotel, LAURIER-GRACHT, Woonbootmuseum, NASSAUKADE, MARNIXSTRAAT, KEIZERS-GRACHT, HEREN-GRACHT, De Negen Straatjes, LEIDSEGRACHT, Keizers-gracht, Heren-gracht, Singel, Bartolotti Huis, RAADHUISSTR, Koninklijk Paleis, SPUISTR, Amsterdam Museum, Bijbels Museum, SPUI, KONINGS-PLEIN, Metz & Co, American Hotel LEIDSEPLEIN, SPIEGEL-KWARTIER, Lijnbaans-gracht, OVERTOOM, Hollandsche Manege ❷, Vondelpark ❸, EERSTE CONSTANTIJN HUYGENSSTRAAT, STADHOUDERSKADE, Rijksmuseum, Van Gogh Museum MUSEUMPLEIN, ❹, ❺ Zuiderbad

❸ Picnic in Vondelpark (see pp. 38, 154–155) One of Europe's best urban green spaces boasts everything you crave in a park, 120 acres (49 ha) of ponds, playgrounds, and picnic areas, and plenty of space to bike, hike, or skate. Exit via the east side of the park, walk along Van Baerlestraat for three blocks, and turn left into Paulus Potterstraat.

**WEEKEND WITH KIDS DAY 2 DISTANCE: 5 MILES (8 KM)
TIME: APPROX. 10 HOURS METRO START: CENTRAAL STATION**

WHIRLWIND TOURS

EYE Film
Institute
Netherlands **6**

BUIKSLOTER-
WEG

DE RUIJTERKADE

Het IJ

Centraal Station

1 Centraal
Station

**Canal
Boat Trip**

ZEEDIJK

De
Schreierstoren

Beurs van
Berlage

Nieuwe
Kerk

Oude
Kerk

**RED-LIGHT
DISTRICT**

PRINS

NEMO

Oosterdok

DAM

OUDEZIJDS VOORBURGWAL

OUDEZIJDS ACHTERBURGWAL

KLOVENIERS-BURGWAL

De Waag

NIEUWMARKT

Montelbaans-
toren

ROKIN

Nieuwmarkt

HENDRIKKADE

Zuiderkerk

Museum het
Rembrandthuis

Allard
Pierson
Museum

Stadhuis-
Muziektheater

Verzetsmuseum

JODENBUURT

Amstel

Hortus
Botanicus

Tuschinski
Theater

Waterlooplein

Joods
Historisch Museum

AMSTEL

BLAUW BRUG

REMBRANDT-
PLEIN

THORBECKE-PLEIN

Museum
Willet-
Holthuysen

Hermitage

NIEUWE KEIZERSGRACHT

Museum van
Loon

MAGERE BRUG

REGULIERSGRACHT

Prinsen-gracht

Amstelkerk

Amstel

FREDERIKSPLEIN

SARPHATISTRAAT

Singelgracht

| 0 | | | 800 meters |
| 0 | | | 800 yards |

6 **EYE Film
Institute Netherlands**
(see p. 39) The EYE offers
both a striking modern building and
an incredible retrospective on more
than a century of moviemaking
from around the world. Visit the
free exhibition in the basement
and catch a flick before taking the
Stromma boat or free ferry back to
Central Station.

5 Zuiderbad (see pp. 39, 168) Decorated with
art deco fountains, waterfalls, and ceramic tiles,
this 100-year-old indoor swimming pool offers
a casual atmosphere year-round. Reboard a
Stromma boat in front of the Rijksmuseum and
enjoy a cruise to the EYE.

4 **Van Gogh Museum** (see pp. 39, 162–165)
Vincent van Gogh's art appeals to people of all
ages, but especially children who delight
in his swirling strokes and bright colors.
Turning right out of the museum, head east
along Paulus Potterstraat and hang a right
onto Hobbemastraat.

GOOD **EATS**

■ DE TROPEN

Soups, salads, and club sandwiches share the menu with dishes from all over the world at this bastion of global cuisine in the Royal Tropical Institute. **Linnaeusstraat 2, 1092 CK, 020 568 2000, €€**

■ EYE BAR-RESTAURANT

Even if you don't lunch or dine at this rooftop café inside the film institute, pop in for one of the wonderful desserts—caramelized pineapple with salted caramel ganache, tiramisu with amaretto, and a white chocolate coffee creme with matcha financier. **IJpromenade 1, 1021 KT, 020 589 1402, €€**

■ T'BLAUWE THEEHUIS

A Vondelpark landmark since 1937, the Blue Teahouse serves a wide range of fresh sandwiches, finger foods, desserts, and drinks for lunch—all in the casual atmosphere of this modernist pavilion at the heart of the park. **Vondelpark, 020 662 0254, €**

Canal Boat Trip

1 Stromma tickets allow unlimited journeys and stops at 8 stations along a watery route that weaves through Amsterdam's canals. Starting from the wharf outside Centraal Station, it cruises down Prinsengracht past several historic houses, including Anne Frank House (with an option to disembark there if you wish).

Prins Hendrikkade 33A, 1012 TM • www.stromma.com • 020 625 3035 • €€€€ • Metro: Centraal Station

Hollandsche Manege

2 Founded in 1744, Holland's leading equestrian school offers riding lessons, an equine gift shop, and tours of its elegant 19th-century stables. The tour of this "living horse museum" includes a video on the school's functions and rich history, as well as a chance for parents to sip tea and coffee. During the fall and summer, the Hollandsche Manege offers pony camps for children of all ages.

Vondelstraat 140, 1054 GT • www.levendpaardenmuseum.nl • 020 618 0942 • €€ • Tram: 1, 11

Picnic in Vondelpark

3 Amsterdam's answer to Central Park is a great place for kids to run about. Rent inline skates at Vondeltuin (*€5 per hour*) and run around Picasso Meadow or the Long Circuit. Eat at one of four cafés or bring your own picnic. During the summer months, watch out for the free plays and concerts staged here. On King's Day (see p. 178) events are geared specifically toward children.

Museumkwartier • www.iamsterdam.com • 020 428 3360 • Tram: 1, 6

Van Gogh Museum

4 Holland's most popular museum showcases more than 200 paintings by the Dutch Postimpressionist master, including self-portraits, sunflowers, and masterpieces like **"The Harvest."** There are also hundreds of drawings, etchings, and personal letters, as well as paintings by Monet, Gauguin, and Toulouse-Lautrec. Kids can try their luck on a van Gogh treasure hunt or create their own colorful canvases during art workshops.

Named, simply, "The Bedroom" (1888), this painting shows van Gogh's bedroom in Arles.

Museumplein 6, 1071 CX • www.vangoghmuseum.nl • 020 570 5200 • €€ • Tram: 2, 3, 5, 11, 12, 19

Zuiderbad

5 Opened around the turn of the 20th century, this indoor swimming pool doubles as an art deco landmark. Although some lanes are marked off for laps, much of the pool is open for playing around. Lockers, showers, and changing rooms available. Be sure to bring a plastic bag to stow your wet suit after swimming.

Hobbemastraat 26, 1071 ZC • www.amsterdam.nl/zuiderbad • 020 252 1390 • €
• Tram: 2, 5, 12

EYE Film Institute Netherlands

6 The stunning new EYE building is a place to explore filmmaking history. More than 10 different films are screened on weekdays and 20 on weekend days, ranging from classics like Charlie Chaplin's *Modern Times* to contemporary icons like *Jurassic Park* (in 3-D).

IJpromenade 1, 1031 KT • www.eyefilm.nl • 020 589 1400 • €€ (movie tickets)
• Closed King's Day • Metro: Centraal Station

PART 2

Amsterdam's Neighborhoods

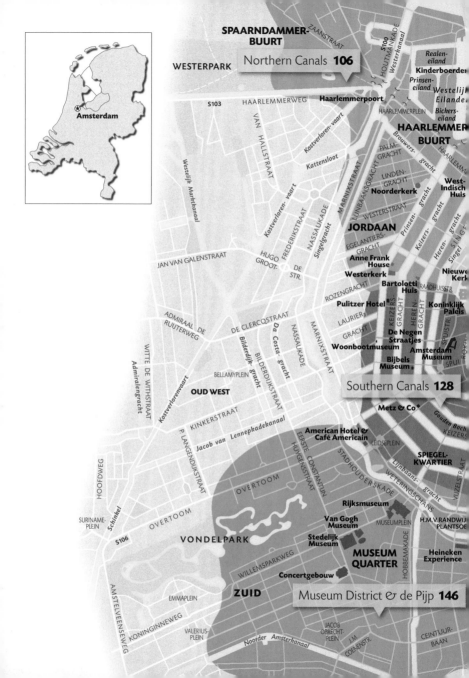

**SPAARNDAMMER-
BUURT**

WESTERPARK

Northern Canals **106**

Haarlemmerpoort

ZAANSTRAAT

S100

HOUTMANKADE

Westerkanaal

*Realen-
eiland*

Kinderboerde

*Prinsen-
eiland*

*Westelij
Eilande*

HAARLEMMERPLEIN

*Bickers-
eiland*

S103

HAARLEMMERWEG

VAN HALLSTRAAT

**HAARLEMME
BUURT**

West-
Indisch
Huis

Brouwers-

PALM-
GRACHT

LINDEN-
GRACHT

Noorderkerk

WESTERSTRAAT

Kostverloren- vaart

Kattensloot

LIJNBAANSGRACHT

MARNIXSTRAAT

gracht

gracht

HAARLEMME

Prinsen-

Keizers-

Heren-

SINGE

Singel

gracht

gracht

gracht

JORDAAN

EGELANTIERS-
GRACHT

**Anne Frank
House**

Westerkerk

**Bartolotti
Huis**

RAADHUISSTR

**Nieuwe
Kerk**

Westelijk Marktkanaal

Kostverloren- vaart

FREDERIKSTRAAT

NASSAUKADE

Singelgracht

HUGO
GROOT-
STR.

DE
STR.

JAN VAN GALENSTRAAT

ROZENGRACHT

Pulitzer Hotel

LAURIER-

GRACHT

KEIZERS
GRACHT

HEREN
GRACHT

**Koninklijk
Paleis**

SPUISTR.

**De Negen
Straatjes**

**Amsterdam
Museum**

SPUI

ADMIRAAL DE
RUIJTERWEG

DE CLERCQSTRAAT

Da Costa-
gracht

Bilderdijk-
gracht

NASSAUKADE

MARNIXSTRAAT

Woonbootmuseum

**Bijbels
Museum**

WITTE DE WITHSTRAAT

Admiralengracht

BELLAMYPLEIN

BILDERDIJKSTRAAT

OUD WEST

Southern Canals **128**

Kostverlorenvaart

KINKERSTRAAT

Metz & Co

Gouden Boch

KEIZERS

HOOFDWEG

P. LANGENDIJKSTRAAT

Jacob van Lennepkadekanaal

EERSTE CONSTANTIJN
HUYGENSSTRAAT

**American Hotel &
Café Americain**

LEIDSEPLEIN

**SPIEGEL-
KWARTIER**

Lijnbaans-

gracht

WETERINGSCHANS

VIJZELSTRAAT

SURINAME-
PLEIN

Schinkel

S106

OVERTOOM

OVERTOOM

STADHOUDERSKADE

VONDELPARK

Rijksmuseum

**Van Gogh
Museum**

MUSEUMPLEIN

H.M.V.RANDWIJ
PLANTSOE

**Stedelijk
Museum**

HOBBEMAKADE

**Heineken
Experience**

**MUSEUM
QUARTER**

WILLEMSPARKWEG

Concertgebouw

ZUID

Museum District & de Pijp **146**

EMMAPLEIN

AMSTELVEENSEWEG

KONINGINNEWEG

VALERIUS-
PLEIN

Noorder Amsterkanaal

JACOB
OBRECHT-
PLEIN

J.M.
COENENSTR.

CEINTUUR-
BAAN

★ **Amsterdam**

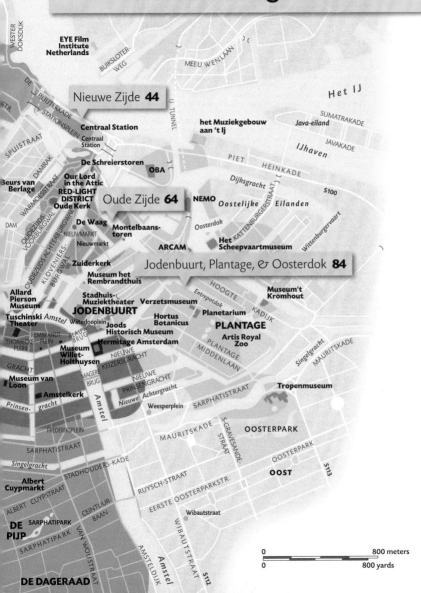

Amsterdam's Neighborhoods

Het IJ

WESTER DOKSDIJK

EYE Film Institute Netherlands

BUIKSLOTER-WEG

MEEUWENLAAN

DE RUIJTERKADE

STR

STATIONSPLEIN

IJ TUNNEL

Het IJ

SUMATRAKADE

Nieuwe Zijde 44

SPUISTRAAT

Centraal Station

Centraal Station

het Muziekgebouw aan 't IJ

Java-eiland

JAVAKADE

DAMRAK

De Schreierstoren

OBA

PIET HEINKADE

Dijksgracht

S100

Beurs van Berlage

WARMOESSTRAAT

Our Lord in the Attic

RED-LIGHT DISTRICT

Oude Kerk

Oude Zijde 64

NEMO

Oostelijke Eilanden

DAM

OUDEZIJDS VOORBURGWAL

De Waag

Oosterdok

Montelbaans-toren

Het Scheepvaartmuseum

Wittenburgervaart

NIEUWMARKT

Nieuwmarkt

ARCAM

KATTENBURGERSTRAAT

OUDEZIJDS ACHTERBURGWAL

Zuiderkerk

Jodenbuurt, Plantage, & Oosterdok 84

KLOVENIERSBURGWAL

Museum het Rembrandthuis

HOOGTE

Entrepotdok

Museum 't Kromhout

Allard Pierson Museum

Stadhuis-Muziektheater

Verzetsmuseum

KADIJK

Tuschinski Theater

Amstel

Waterlooplein

JODENBUURT

Hortus Botanicus

Planetarium

THORBECKE PLEIN

REMBRANDT PLEIN

BLAUW BRUG

Joods Historisch Museum

PLANTAGE

Museum Willet-Holthuysen

NIEUWE KEIZERSGRACHT

Hermitage Amsterdam

PLANTAGE MIDDENLAAN

Artis Royal Zoo

Singelgracht

MAURITSKADE

GRACHT

MAGERE BRUG

NIEUWE PRINSENGRACHT

Museum van Loon

Nieuwe Achtergracht

Tropenmuseum

Prinsen-gracht

Amstelkerk

Amstel

Weesperplein

SARPHATISTRAAT

FREDERIKSPLEIN

MAURITSKADE

S-GRAVESANDE STRAAT

OOSTERPARK

SARPHATISTRAAT

OOSTERPARK

S113

Singelgracht

STADHOUDERS-KADE

OOST

Albert Cuypmarkt

RUYSCH-STRAAT

ALBERT CUYPSTRAAT

CEINTUUR-BAAN

EERSTE OOSTERPARKSTR.

Wibautstraat

DE PIJP

SARPHATIPARK

VAN WOUSTRAAT

WIBAUTSTRAAT

SARPHATIPARK

Amstel

AMSTELDIJK

S112

DE DAGERAAD

| 0 | | 800 meters |
| 0 | | 800 yards |

Nieuwe Zijde

Despite its name—Nieuwe means "new"—this district is no more recent than the neighboring Oude Zijde (Old Side). The two are named after their churches, the Nieuwe Kerk having been built 150 years later than the Oude Kerk. Though altered in many ways today, this western half of Amsterdam's medieval core retains several reminders of its rich past. Heading south from Centraal Station is the district's busy thoroughfare, Damrak. Leading to Dam Square, it follows the course of the Amstel River, which originally divided the inner city in two. The Dam itself started life as a causeway across the river—a link between the two halves of the nascent medieval settlement. Today, the square draws large crowds, not least because it is home to the Nieuwe Kerk and the Koninklijk Paleis (Royal Palace). Crisscrossed by tramlines, waterways, and bicycle lanes, much of this district has been subsumed by commercial development, and yet relief from the hubbub is always close at the Amsterdam Museum, the Begijnhof, and the Bloemenmarkt.

46 Neighborhood Walk

56 In Depth:
    Amsterdam Museum

60 Distinctly
    Amsterdam:
    On Wheels

62 Best Of:
    Secret Amsterdam

◗ Atlas presides over
the vast, marble-lined
Great Hall at the
Koninklijk Paleis.

Nieuwe Zijde

Explore Amsterdam's vibrant past—first in the streets and squares of Nieuwe Zijde and then again at the city's historical museum.

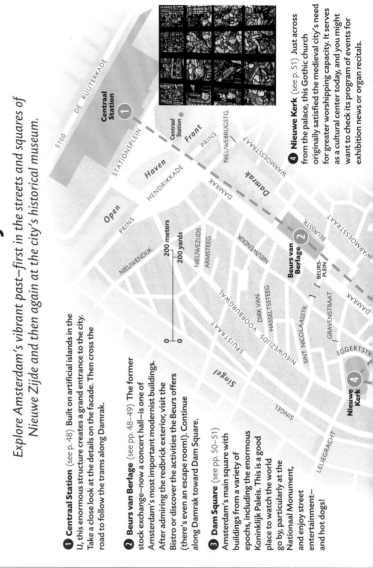

❶ **Central Station** (see p. 48) Built on artificial islands in the IJ, this enormous structure creates a grand entrance to the city. Take a close look at the details on the facade. Then cross the road to follow the trams along Damrak.

❷ **Beurs van Berlage** (see pp. 48–49) The former stock exchange—now a concert hall—is one of Amsterdam's most important modernist buildings. After admiring the redbrick exterior, visit the Bistro or discover the activities the Beurs offers (there's even an escape room!). Continue along Damrak toward Dam Square.

❸ **Dam Square** (see pp. 50–51) Amsterdam's main square with buildings from a variety of epochs, including the enormous Koninklijk Paleis. This is a good place to watch the world go by, particularly at the Nationaal Monument, and enjoy street entertainment—and hot dogs!

❹ **Nieuwe Kerk** (see p. 51) Just across from the palace, this Gothic church originally satisfied the medieval city's need for greater worshipping capacity. It serves as a cultural center today, and you might want to check its program of events for exhibition news or organ recitals.

6 Amsterdam Museum

(see pp. 56–59) From Dam Square head south along the city's busiest shopping street, Kalverstraat, to arrive via Sint Luciensteeg at the entrance to Amsterdam's historical museum. State-of-the-art interactive displays provide a fascinating and comprehensive look at the city's rich past.

5 Koninklijk Paleis

(see pp. 52–53) At the western side of Dam Square, this is the town hall that became fit for a king or queen. Explore the rooms and halls of the palace, where no expense was spared, and look for Atlas, who surveys the Great Hall from the second floor.

7 Begijnhof (see

pp. 53–54) Exit the museum via the Gedempte Begijnensloot and follow it until you reach an archway on the right that leads into the courtyard of the former Beguine convent. Enjoy the peace and quiet as well as its interesting features.

9 Bloemenmarkt

(see p. 55) What better way to end the day, than to take a walk, surrounded by the colors and scents of the floating flower market? Charming and alive with color, it offers a huge choice of flowers, bulbs, and seeds to admire and to buy.

8 **Munttoren** (see pp. 54–55) Continue to the Spui and then back onto Kalverstraat, following it as far as the Mint Tower, one of the city's most recognizable landmarks. Head around the corner to the Singel.

NIEUWE ZIJDE DISTANCE: APPROX. 2.2 MILES (3.5 KM)
TIME: APPROX. 6–7 HOURS METRO START: CENTRAAL STATION

NEIGHBORHOOD **WALK**

GOOD **EATS**

■ **BLUE**
Sandwiches, soups, salads, and hot snacks are standard fare at this smart café. Occupying the top floor of a quirky glass-and-steel structure, it has 360-degree views over the city. **Singel 457, 1012 WP, 020 427 3901, €€**

■ **DE BIJENKORF KITCHEN**
Clean, modern, canteen-style restaurant on the top floor of this department store over-looking Dam Square. Serves a wide variety of hot and cold dishes, with many cooked to order. **Dam 1, 1012 JS, 020 808 9333, €€**

■ **DE DRIE GRAEFJES**
A lovely old café selling light bites, toasted sandwiches, and delicious cupcakes. **Eggertstraat 1, 1012 NN, 020 626 6787, €€**

NIEUWE ZIJDE

Centraal Station

1 One of the city's grandest buildings, Centraal Station is the hub of Amsterdam's transportation network. Running parallel to the shoreline of the IJ River to the north of the medieval city, the location of the station caused controversy when it was built, because it cut off the city from the old harbor that had played a central role in Dutch trade. Be that as it may, the vast redbrick edifice is testimony to the prominence and prosperity of late19th-century Amsterdam. Designed by P. J. H. Cuypers and built between 1891 and 1898, the building stands on artificial islands in the IJ that were created using more than 8,000 wooden piles. Sharing features with the **Rijksmuseum** (see pp. 158–161)—Cuypers' masterpiece across the city—the building is primarily neo-Renaissance in style, with just a smattering of Gothic. With its soaring spires, towers, and carvings, the overall impression is overwhelming, while the ironwork of the shed roofs—one spanning 150 feet (45 m)—is the last word in industrial-age engineering. From the rear of the station, you can take any one of five ferries across the IJ to the north of the city.

Stationsplein, 1012 AB • Tram: 1, 2, 4, 5, 12, 14, 17

Beurs van Berlage

2 The massive Beurs van Berlage building occupies almost one-quarter of the entire length of the Damrak—the avenue that leads from **Centraal Station** to **Dam Square** (see pp. 50–51). Constructed between 1896 and 1903, this mass of red brick, iron, and glass—the city's former stock exchange—was strikingly functionalist in style. So great was its influence on modernist architecture, including the pioneering Amsterdam School movement, that it has long been known and named for its architect, Hendrik Petrus Berlage. At one end of the imposing brick facade stands a landmark clock tower. Look out for the inscriptions, "Await thy hour" and "Bide your time"—an indication, perhaps, that the socialist Berlage was at odds with the capitalist uses for his creation.

At the heart of the building lies the immense trading hall, a multistory space with arched galleries and an iron and glass roof, which is nowadays used for hosting exhibitions and private events. Admission to one of these events will give you access to the hall. Alternatively, you can can sit at the **Bistro Berlage** and enjoy a warm cup of coffee or a cold drink.

Damrak 243, 1012 ZJ • www.beursvanberlage.nl • 020 530 4141 • Metro: Centraal Station • Tram: 2, 4, 12, 14

One of several art nouveau friezes that line the walls of the Beurs van Berlage Bistro

What Dam Square lacks in aesthetics, it makes up for in street art and entertainment.

Dam Square

3 Amsterdam's main public square developed from the earliest days of the city, with the construction of a causeway (dam) across the Amstel (hence the city's name). Just as the Amstel once cut through here, so **Damrak** now divides the square in two. Unlike many other grand squares of Europe, the Dam developed in a piecemeal fashion and has little in the way of architectural homogeneity. It does, however, boast the enormous bulk of the **Koninklijk Paleis** (see pp. 52–53) positioned along its western edge and, across from it, the **Nieuwe Kerk** (see p. 51).

At the eastern end of the square stands the white travertine obelisk of the **Nationaal Monument,** erected in 1956 to commemorate the fallen of World War II. A popular gathering place, it stands at the center of a series of concentric rings that form steps up to the base and is flanked by two lions. The figures on the monument—four males, a woman and child, and two men with dogs—represent war, peace, and resistance. Other prominent buildings in the square include De Bijenkorf department store, which has stood since 1914 on the site of the Beurs van Zocher—predecessor of the **Beurs van Berlage** (see pp. 48–49), and the Peek & Cloppenburg department store, which also houses **Madame Tussauds,** featuring such national and international icons as Michiel Huisman, Ryan Gosling, Taylor Swift, and some of Marvel's heroes in an actual Avengers set (*www. madametussauds.com/amsterdam, 020 522 1010, €€€*).

Intersection of Damstraat and Damrak • Metro: Centraal Station • Tram: 2, 4, 11, 12, 13, 14, 17

Nieuwe Kerk

4 The New Church occupies the northwestern corner of **Dam Square.** Consecrated to St. Catherine and St. Mary, it dates from the early 15th century and was built as a second parish church for the town of Amsterdam when it was realized that the **Oude Kerk** (Old Church; see pp. 71–72) could no longer cope with the rising population. The building was seriously damaged by fire in 1452 and again around 1645. Subsequently rebuilt in the Gothic style we see today, the church has undergone many alterations and renovations in the intervening years. The Nieuwe Kerk now operates primarily as a concert and exhibition space (it offers a variety of events including organ recitals on Christmas and New Year's Day every year). If you pay to visit an exhibition, you can see some of the building's highlights close-up, including the main organ, pulpit, and choir screen. Also of interest are the tombs dedicated to various Dutch naval heroes and a number of commemorative windows. There are also a café and a museum shop.

Commissioned in 1645, the principal organ inside the Nieuwe Kerk was the collaboration of some of the greatest artists living in Amsterdam at the time.

Dam, 1001 AE • www.nieuwekerk.nl • 020 626 8168 • €€€–€€€€ • Closed Jan. 1 and Dec. 25 • Metro: Centraal Station • Tram: 2, 4, 11, 12, 13, 14, 17, 24

NIEUWE ZIJDE

Koninklijk Paleis

5 The most dominant building on **Dam Square,** the Koninklijk Paleis is one of three palaces used by the king for official engagements. Built between 1648 and 1665, it didn't become a royal palace until the early 19th century, however. Following the collapse of the Batavian Republic in 1806, Napoleon Bonaparte installed his brother Louis as king, who took up residence here in 1808. Prior to that, this formidable building served as the town hall.

Working at the height of the Dutch Golden Age, architect Jacob van Campen's task was to create an edifice that reflected the city's prowess in trade, science, and art. The enormous structure is supported on 13,659 wooden piles to keep it from sinking. The sandstone exterior is in French Classicist style, the strict proportions lending it a powerful, almost austere facade. Look up and you'll see its domed cupola topped by a weather vane in the form of a cog ship—the symbol of the city. The facade to the rear is almost more impressive, crowned as it is by an enormous statue of Atlas,

Visitors on a tour of the Koninklijk Paleis are dwarfed by the majestic scale of the Great Hall.

holding the weight of the world on his shoulders. A tour of the rooms and halls within reveals the overwhelming opulence with which they were furnished—there are clocks, chandeliers, paintings, and a huge collection of Empire-style furniture, all left behind by a swiftly departing Louis Napoleon. The highlight here is the 130-foot-long (40 m) **Great Hall,** whose floor features two huge maps of the eastern and western hemispheres, detailing the area of Amsterdam's colonial influence. Throughout the building's lavish marble interior are numerous statues in the classical style. The creations of Flemish sculptor Artus Quellinus, many of them symbolize the nature of the work that went on within the building. Standing before the Magistrate's Court, look up to see a statue of Justice, with skeletal Death to her right and a knee-crusher-wielding Punishment to her left.

Dam, 1001 AM • www.paleisamsterdam.nl • 020 522 6161 • €€ • Metro: Centraal Station • Tram: 2, 4, 11, 12 13, 14, 17

Amsterdam Museum

6 See pp. 56–59.

Kalverstraat 92, 1012 PH | Sint Luciënsteeg 27, 1012 PM • www.amsterdammuseum.nl • 020 523 1822 • €€ • Tram: 2, 4, 11, 12 14, 24

Begijnhof

7 Amsterdam's Beguine convent remains to this day an oasis of calm in the otherwise bustling central part of the city. It was founded in medieval times as a semimonastic institution for widowed and single women—like other similar establishments across the Low Countries. The lay-

Exit the Begijnhof onto the Spui, an elongated square that was filled with water until the 19th century. In medieval times it marked the southern boundary of the city. Today, the shady square is mostly pedestrianized, and it is nice to come here on a Friday for the weekly book market, or for the art market on a Sunday. At the western end is the statue of a small boy, Het Lieverdje (The Little Darling), representing the precocious youth of Amsterdam.

This statue at the Begijnhof serves as a reminder of the women who once lived here. Today, the buildings remain inhabited solely by women.

sisterhood lived under a vow of chastity, helping the local poor. The convent in Amsterdam survived the Protestant Reformation and kept going right up until 1971 when the last Beguine, Sister Antonia, died. You enter through a low arch off the Gedempte Begijnensloot and into a courtyard area covered with an immaculate lawn and lined with houses that have 17th- and 18th-century facades and gables, but are mostly medieval in origin. At the southern end are three buildings that merit closer inspection. **Het Houten Huys** (the Wooden House) dates from about 1425 and is the oldest surviving wooden house in the city. Opposite, in the middle of the courtyard, stands the 14th-century **English Reformed Church.** Formerly the Beguines' chapel, it was confiscated after the Reformation and handed over to English Presbyterians. From then on the Calvinists forbade the Beguines to openly profess their faith; their solution was to join two houses together to create their own **"Secret Chapel,"** which stands adjacent to the Wooden House. Seek out the series of panels within that tell the story of the 1345 Miracle of Amsterdam—an event involving the Holy Sacrament that is celebrated annually in a silent procession through the city's streets (*Stille Omgang, mid-March*).

Nieuwezijds Voorburgwal 373, 1012 RM • www.begijnhofamsterdam.nl • 020 622 1918 • Metro: Rokin • Tram:2, 4, 11, 12, 14

Munttoren

⑧ Standing on the Muntplein where the Singel meets the Amstel River, the Munttoren (Mint Tower) is one of Amsterdam's most recognizable landmarks. The tower dates from 1480, when it formed part of the Regulierspoort gate in Amsterdam's medieval city wall. A fire broke out in 1618, destroying the gate. Only the tower

The Munttoren spire's carillon was made in 1668, but most of the original bells have since been replaced.

and guardhouse were left standing. The tower acquired its name after being temporarily used for minting coins during French occupation in the late 17th century. The bottom half of the tower is original, while the baroque-style top half was added after the fire. Designed by Hendrick de Keyser, the tower features four clock faces and houses a carillon of 38 bells. The bells chime every 15 minutes and, on weekends, visitors can attend a live carillon concert *(Sat. 2–3 p.m)*.

Muntplein, 1012 WR • Metro: Rokin
• Tram: 2, 4, 11, 12, 14

Bloemenmarkt

9 Founded in 1862, stretching from Muntplein along the Singel as far as Koningsplein, this special flower market brings the famous Dutch flower industry right into the heart of the city on a row of floating stalls. Market traders offer a tremendous choice of tulips and other cut flowers, as well as potted plants, bulbs, and seeds. A number of stalls deal in rare plants, such as the black tulip. Before buying bulbs and seeds, however, you should be aware of your country's import restrictions, although vendors are usually able to help with this (and, in some cases, they can organize shipping for you so you don't have to pack your precious bulbs). Souvenirs such as Dutch clogs and wooden tulips are also on sale here.

Open every day of the week, Amsterdam's thriving flower market is a riot of color and sells gardening paraphernalia as well as seasonal blooms.

Singel, bet. Muntplein and Koningsplein
• Metro: Rokin • Tram: 2, 4, 11, 12, 14

Amsterdam Museum

Staged within the labyrinthine layout of a former orphanage,
exhibits tell the story of Amsterdam's diverse evolution.

Centered around an inner courtyard, the museum space was an orphanage for some 300 years.

Visually engaging and thought-provoking, Amsterdam Museum brings to life the vibrant history of the Dutch capital as it traces the city's growth from a tiny fishing village to the thriving metropolis that it is today. The location of the museum—within the 17th-century buildings of the city's former orphanage—only adds to the atmosphere. Augmenting the museum's collection throughout the year are temporary exhibitions on subjects ranging from the Dutch Golden Age to national footballer Johan Cruyff.

■ The Amsterdam Gallery

Your first encounter with the museum will likely be free entry to the **Amsterdam Gallery,** a passageway that runs from Kalverstraat to the **Begijnhof** (see pp. 53–54). Hanging here is an impressive selection of 17th-century group portraits of these defenders of law and order in the city—who also appear in Rembrandt's magnum opus "The Night Watch." However, the first thing that will probably catch your eye is the giant wooden statue of a figure, slowly revolving its head and rolling its eyes. It might look like a modern-day fairground attraction, but in fact it dates from around 1650 when it was commissioned for the city's pleasure garden, Oude Doolhof (Old Maze), no longer in existence. Another unusual exhibit found here is a large painting of Amsterdam, which looks as if it would be more at home in the Louvre. Painted around 1812 by Mattheus Ignatius van Bree, it shows Louis Napoleon (the younger brother of Napoleon Bonaparte) arriving in Amsterdam on horseback. He was king of Holland between 1806 and 1810, during the country's time under French rule.

■ Amsterdam Through the Ages

Once inside the museum proper, you'll find it arranged chronologically, starting from the earliest years of settlement between the 10th and 12th centuries, and Amsterdam's subsequent emergence as a merchant city between 1350 and 1550. As you wander around, keep an eye out for the oldest surviving **map of Amsterdam,** dating from 1538. You will be able to make out the Oude Kerk (see pp. 71–72) and the original dam that blocked off the Amstel River by Dam Square (see pp. 50–51). You'll also be able to see that the Damrak—the busy touristic street leading from Centraal Station to the Dam—is still a canal. The map also gives a good impression of how the city's medieval defenses looked at the time (several of which remain intact to this day). Progressing, a substantial section of the museum considers Amsterdam during

The statue in the Schuttersgalerij represents the biblical figure Goliath.

the 17th century and the flourishing Dutch Golden Age, when trade with the Far East brought immense wealth and power to the city (but recently the museum has also begun to face the darker sides of this period, such as colonialism and its effects). Among the exhibits is a huge map showing those countries from which Dutch merchants imported their herbs and spices during this time. There's also a globe of the world made by a Dutch cartographer in 1640; look closely at it and you will notice that New Guinea and Australia are joined together, as was commonly believed to be the case at that time. See if you can spot the 1685 painting of "**The Bend in the Herengracht, Amsterdam,**" by Gerrit Adriaenszoon

---

SAVVY **TRAVELER**

Kids in tow? Keep them occupied in "Het Kleine Weeshuis" ("The Little Orphanage"), an authentic re-creation of what life would have been like in a 17th-century orphanage. Simply collect a wristband at the museum's reception desk and scan it at the entrance to gain access. You can also use the wristband to activate sounds and stories throughout the exhibition. End with an ice cream at the museum's café. Its courtyard terrace provides a beautiful historic setting and an oasis from the bustling streets surrounding the museum.

Berckheyde. The latter shows one of several views of the Herengracht painted by the artist; the bend it features was known as the Golden Bend (see p. 137), because it was the most expensive section of the canal. The houses in this picture have only just been built, and it is easy to see from this painting just how impressive they were. As you move from one room to the next, it can be fun to compare old images of Amsterdam with the present-day city. "**The Gouden Leeuw on the IJ by Amsterdam,**" for instance, by celebrated marine painter Willem van de Velde the Younger, offers an extraordinary panoramic view of how the harbor looked in 1686. Look beyond the sailing ships to the right, and you'll see the **Schreierstoren** and the **Montelbaanstoren** defenses (see pp. 72–73). George Hendrik Breitner's painting, "**Tram Horses on Dam Square,**" gives us a view of 19th-century Amsterdam. The museum's contemporary collections include technical innovations through the decades and cultural developments, such as the rise of the coffeeshops and gay bars for which the city is famous.

■ Amsterdam DNA

One thousand years of the city's history meets 21st-century technology in this interactive section of the museum.

The museum has an extensive collection of fine, 17th-century Dutch portraits.

Pick up a leaflet with a "personal DNA-CODE" and hold it against the scanners you come across as you walk around. It will activate short films about religion, freedom, tolerance, slavery, and World War II, for instance. Anyone too scared to cycle in Amsterdam can jump on one of two bikes and—as a film of the city's streets plays in front of you—simply pretend.

■ World-City

On the museum's ground floor is the permanent exhibition, World-City, which, as its name implies, explores how Amsterdam sees the rest of the world and how the rest of the world sees it. The exhibition is made even more exciting by the possibility to interact with its components, many of which are multisensorial. For example, visitors can "listen to the paintings," or they can walk along the enlargements of city maps, protected by glass floors, as they get a bird's-eye view of the city's layout.

Kalverstraat 92, 1012 PH | Sint Luciënsteeg 27, 1012 PM • www.amsterdammuseum.nl • 020 523 1822 • €€ • Tram: 2, 4, 11, 12 13, 14, 17

On Wheels

Cycling is an intrinsic part of daily life for the Dutch, and Amsterdam is an excellent example of a city with a sustainability sensibility that designs its transportation system around the bike. Almost 250 miles (400 km) of bike paths wind their way through the city, and, collectively, Amsterdam cyclists travel 1,250,000 miles (2 million km) a day, with an estimated half of all city journeys taking place on two wheels.

Amsterdam's small size, inflated parking fees, and flatness of its terrain contribute to the popularity of the bicycle over the car. Opposite: Public bicycle racks are easily found throughout the city.

Safety First

The Dutch make cycling look easy. A tall, blond, man wearing a suit weaves in and out of traffic, one hand holding up an umbrella against the rain; a student sits nonchalantly on a bike, legs dangling, while her friend peddles; a mother rushes past with a baby and toddler stuffed into seats at either end of her indispensable mode of transportation. Some wear helmets—most do not, because it isn't required by law. Slowly, it will become apparent that common sense and cycling don't always go hand in hand here. Only thanks to an extensive safety campaign (and the threat of being fined) do most of Amsterdam's cyclists now use bike lights at night. And many ignore red traffic lights and cross roads at their peril. You will soon learn that cyclists rule in town, and tourists are considered fair game—wander accidentally into a bike lane and you will be publicly shamed with repeated bell-ringing and probably the odd Dutch expletive . . . or two. Sometimes it's best to give into that old adage: If you can't beat 'em, join 'em.

NIEUWE ZIJDE

Bike Rental

Bright-red "tourist" bicycles from **MacBike** *(www. macbike.nl)* are ubiquitous throughout town in the form of coaster-brake bikes, hand-brake bikes, child bikes, cargo bikes, electric bikes, and tandems. They also, handily, have rental outlets at Centraal Station, Waterlooplein, Vondelpark, Oosterdok, and Leidseplein —and a great selection of maps offering a variety of themed bicycle routes, such as art, architecture, canals and bridges, windmills, and Rembrandt. A less commercial alternative can be found just around the corner from Centraal Station at **Star Bikes Rental** *(www.starbikesrental. com)*. Run by an Australian expat, the store rents out traditional black Dutch bicycles (known as "grandma" and "grandpa" bikes). **Bike City** *(www. bikecity.nl)*, another tourist-friendly establishment in the Jordaan district, has similarly inconspicuous bicycles for rent.

JOY RIDE **TOURS**

A family business run by two American expats, **Joy Ride Tours** *(Keizersgracht 106, www.joyridetours.nl, 06 4361 1798, daily from May to Sept. or May to Oct. for tours tailored to your wishes)* organizes daily cycling adventures with a personal touch for small groups (12 people max.)—either around the city or out into the countryside. They also provide private tours and can create original routes on or off the beaten path to match your wishes. When you've finished pedaling, you and the rest of the group can enjoy an excellent beer in one of the microbreweries if you want.

Secret Amsterdam

As with any major city in the world, Amsterdam does not fall short of the odd secret or surprise. Sometimes they are so obvious that you might walk past them every day without even noticing. Other times, you have to dig a little deeper to find them—or at least know what you're looking for.

■ 1E Klas

Centraal Station (see p. 48), in the Nieuwe Zijde district, holds an unlikely secret. At platform 2B is a swanky café-restaurant called **1e Klas** (*Stationsplein 15, 1012 AB, www. restaurant1eklas.nl, 020 625 0131, €€–€€€*), so-called because it occupies the station's former first-class waiting room. Stepping into its high-ceilinged art nouveau splendor with its smartly dressed waiters is like stepping back in time to the heyday of railroad travel. Keep an eye out for Elvis, the resident cockatoo, who likes to strut up and down the counter.

■ Street Art

There's a chance you'll stumble (literally) across a hand caressing a woman's breast in the cobbled ground of the Oudekerksplein, in the Oude Zijde district, or a headless man running with a violin case on the corner of Marnixstraat and Tweede Hugo de Grootstraat near the Jordaan district. Look closely at one of the older trees in the Leidsebosje, a tiny park near the Leidseplein in the Museum District, and you might notice a tiny statue of a man sawing one of the branches. These statues started appearing around the city in the 1980s and are the work of an anonymous artist. In 1991, on condition of maintaining anonymity, the artist was commissioned to create a work for the City Hall at the Waterlooplein—look for a violinist erupting from the floor! Other street art to look out for are pieces of graffiti by Amsterdam-based **Laser 3.14** or **The London Police,** and the ingenious brown-packing-tape art by **Max Zorn,** which beautifies some of the city's street lights.

■ Cat Boat

Stroll along the Singel canal in the

This anonymous piece nestles in the cobbles of Oudekerksplein in the red-light district.

Northern Canals district and, at mooring 38G, you'll come across a houseboat with curious inhabitants. The **Poezenboot** *(Singel 38G, 1015 AB, www.poezenboot.nl, 020 625 8794, open 1–3 p.m., closed Wed. and Sun.)* is a remarkable volunteer-run refuge for stray and abandoned cats. Pop in and visit the felines. Donations, cat toys, and old newspapers are always welcome.

■ Airport Library & Museum
Amsterdam's Schiphol Airport is home to the world's first airport library *(www.airportlibrary.nl)*, which can be found on Holland Boulevard next to the Rijksmuseum's satellite gallery. Handy if your flight is delayed, the contemporary library offers more than 1,000 Dutch books translated into 30 different languages, plus films on Dutch art and design, which can be viewed on the library's iPads.

You can also visit the Rijksmuseum's auxiliary branch while you wait for your flight or when you land. Displayed in a glass pavilion, the selection of 17th-century paintings from the museum's collection is continuously rotated so that even frequent flyers will always have new works of art to admire.

Oude Zijde

Oude Zijde means "Old Side" and, as the name suggests, this is the oldest part of the city. Its principal canals, Oudezijds Voorburgwal (literally, "in front of the city wall") and Oudezijds Achterburgwal ("behind the city wall"), were dug toward the end of the 14th century, when the area was surrounded by boggy marshland and rising rivers. For centuries, a red-light district has straddled the northern end of these two parallel canals.

The beating neon heart of Amsterdam's historic center, the district's narrow alleyways surround the city's oldest church, the Oude Kerk. The red-lit windows form a peculiar juxtaposition with the venerable building, neatly summing up the area's laissez-faire attitude. Beyond the lights and the ladies, the Oude Zijde turns a different shade of red, as it gently transforms into Chinatown and the former sailor's district, around the Zeedijk. The streets become discernibly quieter and less exotic as they head farther south, into the University Quarter.

66 **Neighborhood Walk**

76 **In Depth: Our Lord in the Attic**

78 **Distinctly Amsterdam: Sex & Drugs**

82 **Best Of: Performing Arts**

◀ **The dome of St. Nicholas Church rises above the old town center. Built toward the end of the 19th century, it is the city's main Catholic church.**

Oude Zijde

*A bustling red-light district and the city's former defenses are among
the highlights of this walk through Amsterdam's historic center.*

1 Zeedijk (see p. 68) Starting at Centraal Station, wind your way south along Zeedijk to Nieuwmarkt square, tracing the course of Amsterdam's medieval city walls.

2 De Waag (see pp. 68–69) Pause to admire this 15th-century weigh house. Exit via the southwest corner of Nieuwmarkt onto the Kloveniersburgwal.

3 Jacob Hooy & Co. (see pp. 69–70) Stop to buy some Dutch licorice from this historic store, then head west to the Oudezijds Achterburgwal, and north into the red-light district.

4 Red-light District (see p. 70) Walk the district's narrow streets and make your way to Oudezijds Voorburgwal. Oude Kerk will come into view. Look out for the statue of "Belle," erected in the church square in honor of the city's prostitutes.

5 Oude Kerk (see pp. 71–72) Having admired Amsterdam's oldest church—both inside and out—retrace your steps to Oudezijds Voorburgwal and head north.

6 Our Lord in the Attic (see pp. 76–77) At no. 40 Oudezijds Voorburgwal, take a tour of Amsterdam's second oldest museum (after the Rijksmuseum). Established in 1888, its attic served as a Catholic church for 200 years. Continue north, back onto the Zeedijk, and onto Oudezijds Kolk.

0   150 meters
0   150 yards

7 De Schreierstoren
(see p. 72) Stop for refreshments at the café in this former defense tower, before strolling down the picturesque Kromme Waal, which leads you onto the Oude Waal.

8 Montelbaanstoren
(see p. 73) After viewing another of the city's defense towers, once sketched by Rembrandt, follow the canal around to the Zuiderkerk.

9 Zuiderkerk (see p. 74)
Head south along the Zwanenburgwal. Turn right at the Staalstraat, and then left onto the Doelenstraat for the Allard Pierson Museum.

10 Allard Pierson Museum (see p. 75)
Complete your tour by exploring ancient civilizations at this archaeological museum—a must for lovers of antiquity and all things mummified.

OUDE ZIJDE DISTANCE: APPROX. 2.2 MILES (3.5 KM)
TIME: APPROX. 5 HOURS METRO START: CENTRAAL STATION

Zeedijk

1 Zeedijk (Sea Dike) runs between Prins Hendrikkade and **Nieuwmarkt** (New Market). It was constructed in the 13th century to protect the medieval city from flooding: Stand on the little bridge by **Oudezijds Kolk** and you can see that it is higher than the streets below. This was originally the sailors' district (the lewd atmosphere of which resonates in Jacques Brel's song, "Port of Amsterdam"). Among the older warehouses on Zeedijk are a number that lean forward at an angle. Their structures were deliberately tilted so that goods did not swing into the building when hoisted up to the balconies of the higher floors. One of only two remaining wooden facades in Amsterdam is at Zeedijk 1—wooden houses were banned after the great fires of 1421 and 1452. Once a sailors' lodgings, the building is currently home to **Café In 't Aepjen** *(020 626 8401, €)*, an authentic beam-ceilinged bar filled with curious monkey paraphernalia. Seamen would pay their drinking tabs by bringing back monkeys from their travels. The place quickly became overrun with flea-ridden monkeys, hence the bar's name—"in the monkeys." As Zeedijk winds toward Nieuwmarkt, you'll notice bilingual street signs, stores selling Chinese wares, and the scent of Asian cuisine from the city's **Chinatown.** Standing out from the neighboring historic houses on either side of the street looms the **Fo Guang Shan He Hua** Buddhist temple *(Zeedijk 106–118).*

www.zeedijk.nl • Metro: Centraal Station or Nieuwmarkt • Tram: 2, 4, 11, 12, 13, 14, 17

De Waag

2 Resembling a fairy-tale castle, the turreted De Waag dominates Nieuwmarkt, a vast square named for its 17th-century function as a marketplace. The building dates from 1456, when it was a gate —Sint Antoniespoort—to the once-walled medieval city. The walls were torn down in 1601 and six years later, the now-extended De Waag became a weigh house. Later, its upper floors were home to the municipal militia and various guilds, such as painters, smiths, and

A weekly farmers market in Nieuwmarkt, with the turrets of De Waag beyond

surgeons. Each guild had its own entrance, marked by stonemasons' reliefs depicting their trade, and these are still visible today. Look up to the central dome, built in 1691, which housed an anatomy theater that carried out dissections, watched by students and the general public. By 1812, the surgeons wouldn't have had to look far for bodies: The Netherlands' first guillotine was installed on scaffolding outside—a remnant from the country's Napoleonic occupation from 1806 to 1810 when the country was under the rule of the French Empire.

Nieuwmarkt 4, 1012 CR • Metro: Nieuwmarkt • Tram: 4, 14

Jacob Hooy & Co.

Despite a 21st-century makeover, this remarkable store, just off Nieuwmarkt, will take you back in time. Having traded in herbs, teas, and spices since 1743, one side of the shop is lined with row upon row of the original wooden barrels containing their wares— each bearing the Latin name of its contents. The store also specializes

NEIGHBORHOOD **WALK**

GOOD **EATS**

■ BIRD
Bird serves delicious Thai food that is well worth standing in line for. Or try its sister snack bar, opposite, at Zeedijk 77. **Zeedijk 74, 1012 BA, 020 620 1442, €€**

■ CAFÉ LATEI
Join the locals at this kitsch café cum bric-a-brac store, which serves some of the healthiest breakfasts and lunches in town. **Zeedijk 143, 1012 AW, 020 625 7485, €**

■ DE BAKKERSWINKEL
A delightful bakery and café offering hearty sandwiches, quiches, scones, cakes—even bacon and eggs for breakfast. **Warmoesstraat 69, 1012 JB, 020 489 8000, €**

in sweet and salty *drop* (Dutch licorice), which soothes sore throats. If you have any ailments, ask for an herbal tea mixture. For other aromatic treats, the modernized part of the shop purveys shampoos, vitamins, and soaps.

Kloveniersburgwal 10–12, 1012 CT • www.jacob-hooy.nl • 020 624 3041 • Metro: Nieuwmarkt • Tram: 4, 14

Red-light District

④ You'll see the odd red-lit window as soon as you enter the world's most famous red-light district. By the time you reach the main strip—the **Oudezijds Achterburgwal**—such windows are flanked by sex shops, sex clubs, and regular bars. It is pretty safe to walk around day and night—especially with all the tourists this area attracts—but do be a little streetwise and look after your belongings. Highlights of the area include **Trompettersteeg**, the narrowest alley in the red-light district, which is akin to walking down the aisle of a superstore. Not for the prudish, the **Erotic Museum** (*Oudezijds Achterburgwal 54, closed Wed., €*) portrays the history of sex and eroticism through the ages. Exhibits include sketches made by John Lennon, including one depicting his and Yoko Ono's weeklong "Bed-in for Peace" at the Amsterdam Hilton in 1969. Changes are underway in this area. Aware of its seedy image abroad, Amsterdam City Council has spent several years trying to rid the red-light district of its criminal element and to quash its less tourist-friendly elements. Having launched Coalition Project 1012 several years ago—1012 stands for the district's postcode—the authorities have actually closed many of the windows and have offered them at price-controlled rents to activities considered more worthy (such as boutiques and bars) but the results have been vacillating.

Metro: Nieuwmarkt • Tram: 4, 9, 16, 24, 25

OUDE ZIJDE

Oude Kerk

5 Dating from the early 13th century, the vast Oude Kerk (Old Church) is so-called because it is the oldest building in Amsterdam. Look at its exterior and you will notice a mishmash of architectural styles from different periods—primarily Gothic below a Renaissance steeple. The land on which the church was built was originally a burial ground. Once inside, you'll see that the uneven floor consists entirely of gravestones. Rembrandt's wife Saskia van Uylenburgh was buried here in 1642, while Rembrandt himself lies in a pauper's grave in the Westerkerk (see p. 111). The medieval, vaulted, wooden ceiling is one of the largest of its kind in Europe. A Latin inscription above the red door into the former sacristy translates as "Marry in haste, repent at leisure." Also of note are the stained-glass windows in the **Lady Chapel** depicting the death of the Virgin Mary,

Some 10,000 people are said to be buried beneath the 2,500 gravestones that pave the interior of the Oude Kerk. The earliest recorded burial is from 1523; the latest, from 1865.

and the **Vater-Müller organ,** built by Christiaan Vater of Hannover between 1724 and 1726. In 1738, when the church tower began to sink, the organ was completely dismantled and later restored by Johan Casper Müller, hence its name. While the organ might still be played for the occasional church service, the Oude Kerk has become a veritable temple to every kind of music. Moreover, it functions as a history museum, a modern art center and a cultural venue. If you visit during the summer months, the church tower is worth a climb for an impressive view *(half-hourly tours from 1–5:30 p.m., €€)*; it is currently closed for renovation, and should be ready for visits again in 2021.

Oudekerksplein 23, 1012 GX • www.oudekerk.nl • 020 625 8284 • €€
• Closed: King's Day and Dec. 25. • Metro: Centraal Station or Nieuwmarkt
• Tram: 2, 4, 14

Our Lord in the Attic (Ons' Lieve Heer op Solder)

6 See pp. 76–77.

Oudezijds Voorburgwal 40, 1012 GX • www.opsolder.nl • 020 624 6604
• €€; tickets include audio tour (see p. 77) • Closed: King's Day • Metro: Centraal
Station or Nieuwmarkt • Tram: 2, 4, 11, 12, 13, 14, 17

De Schreierstoren

7 Like **De Waag** (see pp. 68–69) and **Montelbaanstoren** (see opposite), De Schreierstoren, built circa 1487, formed part of the city's defenses. Its name reputedly means "tower of tears," because this is where weeping women—and probably a few men—bade their farewell to sailors. In fact, the name derives from the old Dutch word *Scrayershoucktoren,* meaning "sharp-cornered tower": You only need to take a look at the building's shape to see why. The tower is most famous for being the point from which English sea captain Henry Hudson set sail in 1609, and discovered what is now New York. Look to the left of the entrance to find a commemorative stone marking this event. The building's primary use today is as a café.

Prins Hendrikkade 94, 1012 AE • Metro: Centraal Station or Nieuwmarkt
• Tram: 2, 4, 11, 12, 13, 14, 17

Montelbaanstoren

8 The Renaissance-style Montelbaanstoren (Montelbaan Tower), built in 1516, sits right on the edge of the **Oudeschans** (Old Rampart), one of Amsterdam's wider canals. As the canal's name suggests, it originally formed part of the city's walled defenses—the city's military guard used it as a lookout for potential invaders. This is also where, in the 17th century, sailors would congregate in small boats before leaving on voyages to far-off lands.

The peculiar three-tiered, white spire, designed by city architect Hendrick de Keyser and with its four identical clock faces, was added in 1606, when the tower ceased to play a defensive role. Both Rembrandt, who lived around the corner, and landscape painter Jacob van Ruisdael chose to portray the brick-walled tower as it was originally—without the spire. The tower contains offices today, but it remains one of the historic city center's most distinctive landmarks.

Oudeschans 2, 1011 KX • Metro: Nieuwmarkt or Waterlooplein • Tram: 14

Malle Jaap—loosely meaning "silly Jack"—became a local nickname for Montelbaanstoren when the newly installed clocks failed to keep time.

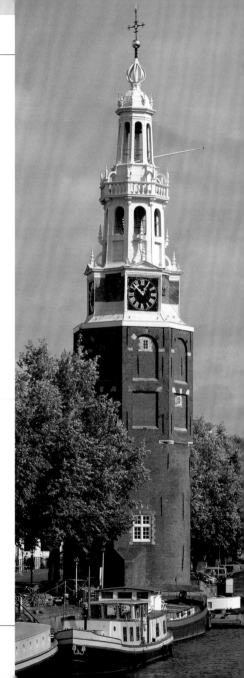

Zuiderkerk

9 It made an impression on Monet—who made an Impressionist painting out of it circa 1874: **"The Zuiderkerk, Amsterdam (looking up the Groenburgwal)."** And it reputedly influenced British architect Christopher Wren in his design for St. Paul's Cathedral in London. Architect Hendrick de Keyser, who built the Renaissance-style Zuiderkerk (Southern Church) between 1603 and 1611, also happens to be buried in the building. It was the first Protestant church of the city. For a while, it was a municipal information center; nowadays, private events and exhibitions take place here.

Zuiderkerkhof 72, 1011WB • www.zuiderkerkamsterdam.nl • 020 308 0399 • Metro: Waterlooplein or Nieuwmarkt • Tram: 9, 14

Zuiderkerk tower rises majestically above Amsterdam's Kloveniersburgwal canal.

Allard Pierson Museum

10 Mummified cats—and even fish—as well as a life-size sarcophagus are among the exhibits at this archaeological museum. Owned by the University of Amsterdam, the museum is named for a celebrated professor of art history who taught at the university from 1877 to 1895. The collection is very much geared toward scholars and researchers. Lovers of antiquity will be rewarded by a superb encounter with the ancient civilizations of Egypt, the Near East, the Greek world, Etruria, and the Roman Empire—all brought to life via art objects and utensils dating from 4000 B.C. to A.D. 500.

Oude Turfmarkt 127, 1012 GC • www.allardpiersonmuseum.nl • 020 525 7300 • €€
• Closed: Mon., Jan. 1, King's Day, and Dec. 25 • Metro: Rokin • Tram: 4, 14

Our Lord in the Attic

*Behind the ordinary facade of a 17th-century
merchant's house lies an extraordinary secret.*

The Sael (parlor) at the heart of the house is furnished handsomely in late-17th-century style.

Bought in 1661 by Jan Hartman, a German hosiery merchant, this canalside
house on the Oudezijds Voorburgwal offers an intriguing insight into life in
Amsterdam following the year of Alteration (see opposite). For in the attic lies
a hidden church in which Catholics could worship covertly when it was forbidden to do so in public. Both the church and the house have been beautifully
preserved; the latter also offers an authentic glimpse into the interior of a
merchant's house during the affluent Dutch Golden Age.

OUDE ZIJDE

■ A Merchant's Home

An informative audio tour provides fascinating snippets about the house (actually three houses joined together), beginning as you walk up the narrow, creaking staircase to the dimly lit rooms. In the **Sael** (parlor), notice how everything is arranged symmetrically, from the way paintings are hung on the wall to the fake door that mirrors the one leading into the room. This interior fashion is typical of the Dutch classical style. Another trend of this era was to sleep in box beds, disguised as cupboards during the day. You can see an example of one in the living room, where you will also find a painting by the landscape painter, Jacob van Ruisdael (1628–1682). In the middle of the house is the Mezzanine, with an additional little room. Walk through to the rear of the house, which was the live-in priest's quarters and includes a preserved 19th-century kitchen with original Delft-blue tiles.

■ Ons' Lieve Heer op Solder

The highlight is, of course, the hidden church spanning the three attics of the adjoining houses, long known as Our Lord in the Attic. Originally, Jan

Hartman built it for his son, who was studying for the priesthood. But in 1671, he rented it out to the Catholic community so they could conduct covert services. To create the spacious three-level church—with its two balconies—the existing beams of two floors were cut through and supported by iron rods, a remarkable feat for its time. Tastefully decorative, it has an altar at one end (look above it for the Jacob de Wit painting, **"The Baptism in the Jordan"**) and an enormous organ at the other, built especially for the church in 1794. Behind the main altar, to the left, is the **Lady Chapel** with an altar dedicated to the Virgin Mary. Walk down the stairs and you'll find the **confessional** where sinners would ask penitence from the priest.

OUDE ZIJDE

Oudezijds Voorburgwal 40, 1012 GX • www.opsolder.nl • 020 624 6604 • €€; tickets include audio tour • Closed: King's Day • Metro: Centraal Station or Nieuwmarkt • Tram: 2, 4, 11, 12, 13, 14, 17

Sex & Drugs

Even if you are only here out of sheer curiosity, Amsterdam's red-light district—or De Wallen, as it is known colloquially—should not be missed. This is especially true at night, when the neon signs of sex clubs and the red-lit windows reflect off the canals, making it strangely picturesque. This is arguably the city's main tourist attraction, although the coffeeshops purveying marijuana by the gram are another big draw.

The narrow alleyways of the red-light district are lined with around 200 red-lit windows, from which prostitutes advertise themselves and the various services they have on offer.
Opposite: The Erotic Museum

Clean Streets

Since the launch of Coalition Project 1012 (see p. 70), Amsterdam City Council has closed down many of the district's red-lit windows and its most notorious brothel, Yab Yum. However, most visitors probably wouldn't notice. The sex business continues as usual, day in and day out.

Working Girls

With the Dutch prostitution model, you won't find women walking deserted streets late at night, waiting for a car to slow down. Instead, scantily clad women of all shapes, sizes, and nationalities—including transsexual women—confidently vie for business from the illuminated windows of variously gabled 17th- and 18th-century houses. These women look out for each other, the CCTV cameras keep a constant eye on activity, and, at the first sign of any trouble, the women can sound an alarm. Amsterdam also has a Prostitutes Union for the working girls and, for visitors, a Prostitution Information Center

OUDE ZIJDE

(Enge Kerksteeg 3, www.pic-amsterdam.com, 020 420 7328), founded by a former sex worker. Here you can find out more about the working life of the women in Amsterdam. You can also book a tour of the district, given in English *(Wed.–Sat., 5 p.m., €€, 4 people max.)*, and buy books or a miniature version of Belle (see p. 66). The world's oldest profession was legalized in Amsterdam in 2000, meaning that the self-employed prostitutes also pay tax on their earnings.

When window-shopping in this utterly unique district in the world, be sure to show respect toward the women. Never photograph them (your camera may end up in the water), and if you want to take a general shot of the red-lit windows, it is advisable to do so discreetly.

FILM **CHOICE**

For an authentic insight into life inside De Wallen, keep an eye out for the bittersweet documentary, **Meet the Fokkens** (2011). It follows the lives of Amsterdam's most famous prostitutes—the 69-year-old identical twins, Louise and Martine Fokkens—as they go about their daily business, reminisce about World War II, and turn their hand to painting.

OUDE ZIJDE

Pot Laws

It is not actually legal to buy or smoke cannabis in
Amsterdam. However, thanks to the liberal Dutch attitude
toward soft drugs, it has been decriminalized. This means
that police turn a blind eye to anyone over the age of 18
smoking a joint or buying a small amount of cannabis, as
long as it weighs less than 5 grams. In fact, there was uproar
in the ranks in 2008, when senior members of Amsterdam's
police force penned a missive warning their officers not to
smoke cannabis off-duty! In truth, the country's right-wing
politicians are not fond of drug tourism, despite the fact that
it swells the tax coffers annually by around 400 million euros.
In 2012, the government tried to introduce a "weed pass,"
which would allow only Dutch residents the right to go into

"coffeeshops." Although it was enforced in the south of the country, it was eventually scrapped. Another threat came from the nationwide tobacco ban in 2008, when it was no longer permitted to smoke in bars or restaurants. Amsterdam's 220 coffee shops were forced to create airtight "smoking rooms" in their already tiny premises and bring in the bongs and vaporizers—a move that created a seismic panic around the globe. The regulation still stands and many have changed to "pure" joints inside the coffee shops.

Pot Luck

Amsterdam's regular cafés are not to be confused with its coffeeshops. The former, often referred to as *bruine* (brown) cafés, are local establishments that serve tea, coffee, alcoholic drinks, and snacks. Traditionally, they have dark, wooden interiors— the walls colored by decades of cigarette-smoking customers—and a laid-back, friendly atmosphere. No less convivial, Amsterdam's coffeeshops differ in that they also sell soft drugs. And because these establishments are not allowed to advertise their wares, you could easily walk into one without even realizing it. The odd waft of smoke may be the only clues. Once inside a coffeeshop, you can order tea, coffee, or soft drinks, salty snacks such as chips, and there's usually a menu with different kinds of hash (resin) and weed (grass), which you can buy by the gram or as ready-rolled joints. If you want to find out more about cannabis, such as its history and medicinal usage—and see Nike and Adidas sneakers made from hemp—head to the **Hash, Marihuana, & Hemp Museum** (*Oudezijds Achterburgwal 148, 1012 DV, www.hashmuseum. com, 020 624 8926, €, closed King's Day*).

Visitors to the Hash, Marihuana, & Hemp Museum can expect to find the world's largest collection of artifacts relating to the history of cannabis, its cultivation, and its uses over the centuries. Opposite: The Headshop, selling drug paraphernalia

Performing Arts

Whether you are looking for highbrow theater, world-class ballet, or an underground nightclub, Amsterdam has a diverse and thriving arts program and is especially strong on avant-garde work. Long-standing theaters and live-music venues provide year-round entertainment for all budgets—night and day.

■ Nes

Amsterdam's theater street, Nes, is just a short walk from the red-light district. Among the attractions, Flemish arts center **De Brakke Grond** (*Nes 45, www. brakkegrond.nl, 020 626 68 66, €€€*) often stages shows and exhibitions, with a specific focus on Flemish artists, which are accessible to English speakers.

Nes, 1012 KD • Tram: 4, 14

■ Dutch National Opera & Ballet

In-house companies, De Nederlands Opera and Het Nationale Ballet, give

Concertgebouw plays host to as many as 900 concerts per year.

terrific performances throughout the year in the heart of Jodenbuurt. Past events from an excellent international program include a concert by Icelandic singer Björk and an opera by Chinese composer Tan Dun.

Amstel 3, 1011 PN • www.operaballet.nl • 020 551 8117 • €€€€ • Metro: Waterlooplein • Tram: 14

■ International Theatre Amsterdam

"Stunning, with a capital S," is how Cate Blanchett described the work of Ivo van Hove, the artistic director of ITA-Ensemble, the country's largest repertory company. Based here, in the Southern Canals district, they sometimes perform their plays with English supertitles.

Leidseplein 26, 1017 PT • www.ssba.nl • 020 624 2311 • €€€€ • Tram: 1, 2, 5, 6, 7, 10

■ Melkweg

A former dairy—hence its name, Milky Way—this multimedia venue has a cinema, theater, photography gallery, and two concert halls programming everything from pop and punk to post-rock and club nights. In 2009, a brand-new concert hall was built connecting the Melkweg with the adjacent municipal theater, **Stadsschouwburg**. It was while waiting to go on stage here that Coldplay's Chris Martin penned the song "Amsterdam" (2002).

Lijnbaansgracht 234a, 1017 PH • www.melkweg.nl • 020 531 8181 • €€€ • Tram: 1, 2, 5, 7, 11, 12, 19

■ Concertgebouw

Extraordinary acoustics and a rich repertoire of world-class conductors and orchestras define this palatial, classical music venue, which first opened in 1888. Based in the Museum District (see pp. 151–153), it is one of the busiest venues of its kind in the world. To sample its magnificence and quality, line up alongside erudite Amsterdammers for the free lunchtime concerts every Wednesday (except in July and August). Evening concert tickets usually include a couple of glasses of wine.

Concertgebouwplein 10, 1071 LN • www.concertgebouw.nl • 020 573 0573/020 671 8345 (ticket service) • €€€€€ • Tram: 2, 11, 12

■ Comedy Café

In cabaret performances in English and Dutch, stand-up comedians put on their shows, generally from Thursday through Saturday, while open mic nights usually take place from Monday through Wednesday.

IJdok 89 1013 MM • www.comedycafe.nl • 020 722 0827 • €€ • Metro: Centraal Station

Jodenbuurt, Plantage, & Oosterdok

Jodenbuurt (the "Jewish neighborhood") is the area centered around Waterlooplein, formerly an island. It was here, circa 1600, that the first Jewish refugees settled. Remnants of this once-Jewish enclave are still visible: There's the Jodenbreestraat; some stunning 17th-century synagogues; and Waterloopleinmarkt, with its origins in Jewish street trade. More affluent citizens gravitated toward the adjacent Plantage, a verdant area with botanical gardens, a zoo, small parks, and centuries-old trees. North of both districts is the Oosterdok (Eastern Dock), where maritime history rubs shoulders with urban regeneration.

86   **Neighborhood Walk**

96   **In Depth:
Museum het
Rembrandthuis**

98   **Distinctly
Amsterdam:
The Nazi Occupation**

102 **Best Of:
Street Markets**

❰ **A life-size replica of a Dutch East India Company cargo ship is moored in Oosterdok. Laden with textiles, wine, and silver, she was wrecked in 1749.**

Jodenbuurt, Plantage, & Oosterdok

This diverse tour celebrates Amsterdam's Jewish history, its maritime traditions, and its inner-city flora and fauna.

❶ Museum het Rembrandthuis (see pp. 96–97) Visit the studio in which Rembrandt painted his magnum opus, "The Night Watch." On leaving, walk down the little passage on the right to the start of the Waterlooplein markt.

❷ Waterlooplein markt (see pp. 88, 102) Seek out a bargain at Amsterdam's flea market, then cross the road by the huge, white-spired Moses and Aaron Church onto the Weesperstraat. Head down the next alleyway on the right.

❽ Het Scheepvaartmuseum (see pp. 94–95) A treat for all, this 17th-century naval building portrays 500 years of maritime history. After wandering through it, board the full-scale replica of the 18th-century merchant ship moored in the dock outside.

OOSTERDOKSKADE

Centraal Station

PRINS HENDRIKKADE

Oosterdok

Oosterdok

Rapen- burgwal

Amsterdam

❽ Het Scheepvaartmuseum

KATTENBURGER-PLEIN

Nieuwevaart

NIEUWEVAART

WITTENBURGER-GRACHT

KLEINE WITTENBURGER STRAAT

GROTE WITTENBURGER STRAAT

Kattenburgervaart

VALKENBURGER STRAAT

RAPENBURGER PLEIN

ANNE

NIEUWE UILENBURGERSTRAAT

SINT ANTONIESLUIS

JODENBUURT

Museum het Rembrandthuis 1

Waterlooplein 2

3 Joods Historisch Museum (see pp. 88–89) Brush up on Jewish culture and history, then cross the road to the striking Portuguese Synagogue. From Jonas Daniël Meijerplein, turn left by the water and cross the bridge onto the Plantage Middenlaan.

Joods Historisch Museum 3

Hortus Botanicus 4

Hollandsche Schouwburg 5

Verzetsmuseum 6

Artis Royal Zoo 7

200 meters
200 yards

7 Artis Royal Zoo (see pp. 93–94) Arrive in time to watch the lions feeding, or to stroke a giant tortoise, during one of several zookeeper talks. Turn left after the bridge, following the canal around onto the Kadijksplein. Walk to the end and the Scheepvaartmuseum will come into view.

5 Hollandsche Schouwburg (see pp. 91–92) It was from here that most of Amsterdam's Jewish population started its deportation to the concentration camps. Cross over the road to read the plaque at Plantage Middenlaan 31, then turn left down the Plantage Kerklaan.

4 Hortus Botanicus (see pp. 90–91) Relax in one of the world's smallest botanical gardens. Then continue down the street to No. 24, making a quick detour to the park opposite to see the Auschwitz Monument (1993), made up of broken mirrors.

6 Verzetsmuseum (see pp. 92–93) Explore this interactive museum to get a feel for how life in Amsterdam must have been under German occupation during World War II. Step across the road to enter the zoo.

JODENBUURT, PLANTAGE, & OOSTERDOK

JODENBUURT, PLANTAGE, & OOSTERDOK DISTANCE: APPROX. 1.2 MILES (2 KM) TIME: APPROX. 8 HOURS TRAM START: WATERLOOPLEIN

Museum het Rembrandthuis

1 See pp. 96–97.

Jodenbreestraat 4, 1011 NK • www.rembrandthuis.nl • 020 520 0400
• €€ • Metro: Waterlooplein or Nieuwmarkt • Tram: 14

SAVVY **TRAVELER**

Nip back to Waterloopleinmarkt when the stallholders are packing up at around 5 p.m., for some last-minute bargains—one market trader's trash could become your treasure.

Waterloopleinmarkt

2 The colorful market stalls pitched along the Amstel canal mark the start of the world-famous flea market that takes its name from the square it occupies, **Waterlooplein.** Originally this was the site of a Jewish market, established in 1893, but that ceased to exist during German occupation. Trade resumed after World War II, however, with the market experiencing a heyday in the 1960s and 1970s (see p. 102).

Waterlooplein, 1011 NV • www.waterlooplein.amsterdam • Closed Sun.
• Metro: Waterlooplein or Nieuwmarkt • Tram: 14

Joods Historisch Museum

3 The Jewish Historical Museum is housed in a complex made up of four former Ashkenazi synagogues. Once you've picked up the free audio tour (visitors are required to bring their own headphones), follow the blue signs through the maze-like museum to the **Great Synagogue**—the earliest and most prestigious of the four—which dates from 1671. This will lead you to the start of the permanent exhibition, which provides a background on the religion, by way of torahs and menorahs, plus films explaining traditional Jewish customs. Don't miss the small room marked **Art Gallery,** just off the main room, where you'll find a ritual bath *(mikveh)* that was in use here between 1671 and 1823, but was only discovered as recently as 1987 during restoration work. Back in the synagogue, walk up the spiral staircase to the upper floor, which displays four centuries of history from 1600, when the first groups of Jews settled in tolerant Amsterdam. The adjacent **New Synagogue** gives a vibrant account of Jewish life in the Netherlands before, during, and after World War II, supported by artifacts, interviews, photographs, and documents. Film footage includes images of Jewish cultural hub, the Tuschinski theater, shot between 1930 and 1935, and the demolition in 1966 of Westerbork transit camp where Jews were held before being put on trains bound for Auschwitz, Sobibór, Theresienstadt, or Bergen-Belsen. The museum stages engaging temporary exhibitions throughout the year, and there's an interactive **Children's Museum** centered around a typical modern Jewish family living in Amsterdam. Admission to the museum includes free entry to the 17th-century **Portuguese Synagogue** across the road.

Nieuwe Amstelstraat 1, 1011 PL • www.jhm.nl • 020 531 0310 • €€ • Closed King's Day, Rosh Hashanah, and Yom Kippur • Metro: Waterlooplein • Tram: 14

The floor of the Portuguese Synagogue is dusted with sand to absorb noise, dirt, and moisture.

Hortus Botanicus

4 As you walk through the gates of one of the world's oldest botanical gardens, you'll immediately feel a sense of serenity. The Hortus is the verdant heart of Amsterdam and although relatively small, there's plenty to explore. It originated in a medicinal herb garden founded by the city council in 1638 after Amsterdam had experienced a plague. It grew rapidly over the next 160 years, thanks to the ships of the Dutch East India Company, which came back laden with herbs, spices, and exotic plants. In 1706, the Company brought back coffee seeds from Jakarta, which were cultivated in the greenhouses here. Some of the resulting plants were taken to Central and South America and were responsible for the continent's coffee culture.

Pick up a map at the entrance so you don't miss anything. First stop will be the **Orangery,** originally a place for storing citrus fruits, then a lecture hall, and now an outdoor café. In the adjacent three-climate greenhouse, a raised walkway takes you high above the plants in a hot subtropical section and through a warm, humid tropical

Curvaceous forms, added in 1863, intentionally distract visitors from their urban surroundings.

section—it's like being in a jungle. That then leads into a warm, dry desert area, full of cacti. Stroll through a peaceful garden to the Victorian-style 1912 **Palm House**—home to an Eastern Cape giant cycad that is more than 300 years old—and then on to the **Butterfly Greenhouse.** Dozens of colorful butterflies will flutter all around you in this small 1896 construction. You can even watch them emerge from their pupae here. Head to Hortus on a Sunday afternoon for a free one-hour tour of the garden and its greenhouses (*2 p.m., given in Dutch*).

Plantage Middenlaan 2A, 1018 DD • www.dehortus.nl • 020 625 9021 • € • Closed Jan. 1 and Dec. 25 • Metro: Waterlooplein • Tram: 14

Hollandsche Schouwburg

5 An impressive neoclassical building, the Hollandsche Schouwburg opened in 1892 and was, at the time, the city's largest and most luxurious theater. However, in 1942, during Nazi occupation, it took on a sinister role as a deportation center for Jews. Most were brought here by force and, once registered, children were separated from their parents and taken to a crèche opposite, at No. 31 Plantage Middenlaan, while anguished parents awaited their fate in miserable conditions. Those children who weren't smuggled out (see pp. 100–101) ended up in concentration camps. Today, there is little left of the gutted theater, but its facade and marble entrance give an impression of its former grandeur. Now a monument and war memorial, it has a modest free-entry museum on the first floor with photos, videos, and various objects detailing the persecution of Jews between 1940 and 1945, as well as a small display on the theatrical history of the building. Lining the walls of the staircase are family photographs depicting Jewish life before, during, and

GOOD **EATS**

■ **BABEL**
A restaurant on the seventh floor of Amsterdam's public library, offering healthy soups, salads, and ciabattas. Ask them to stone-bake a pizza or cook a stir-fry to order. Great views. **Oosterdokskade 143, 1011 DL, 020 523 09 31, €€**

■ **BURGERMEESTER**
Trendy joint opposite the entrance to Artis Royal Zoo, selling traditional burgers made with local, seasonal ingredients. Try the Burger of the Month. **Plantage Kerklaan 37, 1018 CV, 088 287 4377, €**

■ **TISFRIS**
Bright, light, colorful café, with friendly staff and a great terrace on the bridge by Rembrandthuis and Waterlooplein. Healthy food. **Sint Antoniesbreestraat 142, 1011 HB, 020 622 0472, €**

JODENBUURT, PLANTAGE, & OOSTERDOK

IN **THE KNOW**

On March 25, 1943, Jewish prisoner Willie Alexander described the bleak conditions in the makeshift deportation center in his wartime diary: "There are presently 1,300 people packed into the Hollandsche Schouwburg. It's so hot and stuffy in here (and of course stinks!) that people just keep on asking for water and more water. The only ones who have a mattress to sleep on are the old women, others as an exception. For all these 1,300 people, there are only two toilets for the men and three for the women."

after World War II. On the ground floor is the **Wall of Remembrance,** with 6,700 surnames representing the 104,000 Jews from the Netherlands who perished in the Holocaust. Look down on the floor and you will see an eternal flame burning (see p. 100). Little remains of the courtyard—formerly the auditorium—not least its roof, but its tragic past is almost tangible. At the back is a memorial column that rests on a Star of David. Behind this, engraved onto the wall, are the words: *Ter herinnering aan hen die van hier werden weggevoerd*—In memory of those who were taken from this place. The building is currently undergoing renovation, which will be finished in 2022. The goal is to unify this Memorial and the National Holocaust Museum (also closed for renovation) in order to better commemorate those who lost their lives and gather the evidence of the persecution of the Jewish population.

Plantage Middenlaan 24, 1018 DE • www.hollandscheschouwburg.nl • 020 531 0340 • Closed King's Day, Rosh Hashanah, and Yom Kippur • Metro: Waterlooplein • Tram: 14

Verzetsmuseum

6 The Resistance Museum is housed in a striking neoclassical building that was built circa 1875 to house the Jewish choral society, Oefening Baart Kunst (Practice Creates Art). Look up and you'll see a Star of David on its facade. It is hard to imagine that this grand building was later used as a taxi garage and—somewhat ironically—was where German occupiers parked their vehicles at the end of World War II. At this museum, you can get a real feel for what life was like for the Dutch during the wartime occupation. Arranged in chronological order, the exhibition starts with a section devoted to the Netherlands in the 1930s. It then seamlessly moves into the five-year occupation from May 1940, ending with the liberation in May 1945 by allied forces, and the postwar years. An additional section of the exhibition covers the story of Japanese occupation of the Dutch East Indies (Indonesia) from 1941 to 1942—look for the story of a dog named Wolf.

The interactive permanent exhibition brings history to life in a vivid way. You can change film clips by holding your hand against a screen, flip over the pages of a book to cue audio stories, peek through peepholes, and open doors and drawers. The exhibits are translated into English, plus there's a free audio tour available. Both educational and poignant, exhibits include film footage of Hitler's blitz of Rotterdam, which drew the previously neutral Netherlands into the war; small broadcasting cases brought along by the secret agents who had been parachuted in; and the identity card of a male student who was forced to assume a female identity in order to survive. In October 2013, a dedicated children's museum opened on the site.

A drill monkey. Artis Royal Zoo's full name, Natura Artis Magistra, means "nature, the teacher of art."

Plantage Kerklaan 61, 1018 CX • www.verzetsmuseum.org • 020 620 2535 • €€ • Closed Jan. 1, King's Day, and Dec. 25 • Metro: Waterlooplein • Tram: 9, 14

Artis Royal Zoo

7 Artis isn't just a zoo, it's a historical site whose grounds are full of beautiful buildings and monuments dating from 1838 when the zoo was founded. It is also home to an oak tree that was planted around 1760 (you'll find it

SAVVY **TRAVELER**

Although Artis opened in 1838, it was originally members-only. When it opened to the public in 1851, the masses were admitted only in the month of September. To this day, September remains discount month, with the hefty entrance fees reduced by 25 percent.

near the chimpanzee enclosure). In 1883, it was in this zoo that the quagga became extinct after living here for 16 years. It had the misfortune of resembling a zebra, and the Dutch didn't realize it was actually a rare subspecies of the striped animal until it was too late.

Whether or not you approve of zoos, this is perhaps one of the better ones you'll visit. The more traditional, Victorian-style iron cages are eschewed—except for the big cats and gorillas—making way for low walls, fences, and moats. It feels open and more like a miniature wildlife park despite its relatively compact size. A visual, aural, and—occasionally—olfactory assault, the zoo is home to more than 900 species of animal, ranging from elephants, giraffes, and gorillas to less well-known creatures, including the Macleay's spectre stick insect, pygmy marmoset, and burrowing owl—what Artis terms the forgotten animals. The layout is maze-like—especially with all the greenery—so be sure to arm yourself with a map at the entrance, then wander through at your leisure. And when you feel like a break, picnic at one of many quiet spots or pause for breath at one of its cafés. On the same site are an **Aquarium, Butterfly Pavilion, Insectarium,** and **Planetarium.**

Plantage Kerklaan 38–40, 1018 CZ • www.artis.nl •020 523 3670 • €€€
• Metro: Waterlooplein • Tram: 14

Het Scheepvaartmuseum

8 Before entering the National Maritime Museum, take time to admire the historic building in which it is housed. Erected in 1656, it served as an arsenal and was used for storing cannon, sails, flags, and other naval equipment. Once inside, you can explore 500 years of maritime history via a number of interactive exhibitions. Among numerous models and paintings of ships and other nautical

paraphernalia, there are several, often unexpected, highlights. These include an inspired exhibition on the whaling trade, which begins with a whale's open maw and ends as the whale's tail disappears into the water. Meanwhile, a 65-foot (20 m) model of the port of Amsterdam affords an insight into the daily workings of Europe's fourth largest port. Once you have wandered through the exhibits, don't miss the full-size replica of the *Amsterdam,* moored alongside the museum. An 18th-century merchant ship of the Dutch East India Company, it sank off the coast of England during a storm on its maiden voyage. Visitors can climb on board and go below deck to take a peek at the galley, the captain's cabin, and the cramped sleeping quarters of the sailors. It gives a vivid impression of life aboard a ship during the Golden Age of Dutch supremacy in European trade, science, and the arts.

Kattenburgerplein 1, 1018 KK • www.hetscheepvaartmuseum.nl • 020 523 2222 • €€ • Closed Jan. 1, King's Day, and Dec. 25 • Metro: Centraal Station • Bus: 22, 48

Het Scheepvaartmuseum sits on one of the artifical islands that make up Oosterdok.

Museum het Rembrandthuis

Explore Rembrandt's 17th-century home, marvel at his etchings, and discover how financial problems were the ruin of this great artist.

Within the permanent collection are pieces by artists working in Amsterdam in the early 1600s.

Built in 1606, the year in which Rembrandt van Rijn was born, this attractive shuttered house was where the Dutch artist lived from 1639 to 1658, after which bankruptcy forced him to leave. It was thanks to the inventory of his household goods and possessions for auction, however—along with many of his own drawings and etchings—that experts were able to reconstruct the interior. The museum (with its excellent free audio tour) not only provides a vivid picture of the artist, but also of life in 17th-century Holland.

Who Was Rembrandt?

In the museum you will encounter not only Rembrandt the painter, but also the man, the collector, and the entrepreneur.

17th-Century Interior Design

The museum houses a collection of Rembrandt's etchings and prints, as well as a number of paintings by other artists. As you tour its rooms, consider the furnishings as well as the art. Notice how short the box beds are in the living room and anteroom. Back then, the superstitious Dutch would sleep sitting up, since they associated lying down with death. Look closely at the marble fireplace in the anteroom—part of it is genuine marble, the rest is wood painted with a marble effect.

Rembrandt the Art Collector

Rembrandt was not only an artist, but also an art collector. If his house had ever gone up in flames, he would undoubtedly have grabbed his art books, which contained around 8,000 drawings and prints including work by Titian, Hans Holbein, and Michelangelo. Among the paintings in the permanent exhibition are a number by Pieter Lastman, Rembrandt's teacher in Amsterdam.

Rembrandt and the Elephant

In 1637, a young albino elephant was brought to Amsterdam from Ceylon and was the subject of a wonderful pencil drawing by a fascinated Rembrandt. The elephant even made an incongruous appearance in Rembrandt's etching, **"Adam and Eve in Paradise"** (1638). Exhibits of his etchings rotate, but see if you can find it. If not, a gablestone celebrating this famed elephant is on a wall at Nieuwe Batavierstraat 2, just a short walk from the museum.

SAVVY **TRAVELER**

Head to Sint Antoniesluis (St. Anthony Sluice) opposite Rembrandthuis for a wonderful view of another of his subjects—**Montelbaanstoren** (see p. 73). The sluice itself dates from 1695, but appeared in its former incarnation in a drawing of Rembrandt's dating from the mid-17th century. The café beside the sluice, which leans a little unnervingly to one side, used to be the sluicemaster's home.

JODENBUURT, PLANTAGE, & OOSTERDOK

Jodenbreestraat 4, 1011 NK • www.rembrandthuis.nl • 020 520 0400 • €€ • Metro: Waterlooplein or Nieuwmarkt • Tram: 14

The Nazi Occupation

Fleeing persecution, the first groups of Jews settled in Amsterdam around 1600: The wealthy Sephardic Jews—hailing predominantly from Portugal and Spain—and the impoverished Ashkenazi Jews from Central and Eastern Europe. Even then, Amsterdam was renowned for its tolerance and religious freedom and the new arrivals could practice their beliefs without any fear. They weren't to know how all that would change almost overnight on May 10, 1940.

JODENBUURT, PLANTAGE, & OOSTERDOK

DIGITAL **MONUMENT**

Established in 2001 by Professor Emeritus Isaac Lipschits and maintained by the **Joods Historisch Museum,** this website *(www.joodsmonument. nl)* is a tribute to the Jewish community in Amsterdam and the rest of the Netherlands. The homepage is made up of tiny squares, each representing a man, woman, or child who died in the Holocaust. Clicking on them reveals personal details of the victims: when they were born, where they died, how they died, and where they had lived. It is a sobering but insightful experience.

The Final Solution

On that day, German troops marched into the Netherlands and occupied the previously neutral country as World War II raged on. With them, they brought sinister Nazi ideology. On February 22, 1941, they organized the first large-scale deportation of Jews. Within a year, they had turned Westerbork—set up in 1939 to handle the large number of Jewish refugees arriving from Germany—into a transit camp. From here, Jews were packed into trains to endure the hellish journey to Auschwitz and other concentration camps more than 700 miles (1,100 km) away.

Jewish Life in Amsterdam

Since the turn of the 20th century, Amsterdam's 80,000-strong Jewish population had enjoyed a relatively emancipated and carefree existence. Now, under German occupation, life became grim. Once stalwarts of the entertainment industry, Jews were no longer allowed to enter theaters, restaurants, cinemas, or even parks. And they were not allowed to travel on trams. They were dismissed from government and public offices, and forced to leave hospitals. They had to observe a strict curfew (8 p.m. to 6 a.m.) and wear a yellow Star of David, bearing the word *Jood* (Jew), at all times—even inside their own homes. Many went into hiding—some in animal enclosures at Artis Royal Zoo. The most famous of these was, of course, Anne Frank (see pp. 118–121). She, and others like her, were aided by brave members of the Dutch resistance.

The Cost to the Community

Before World War II, there had been a thriving community of around 130,000 Jews living in the Netherlands (80,000 in Amsterdam alone). After 1945, there were just 30,000. Of the 25,000 or so Jews who had gone into hiding, some 7,000 perished. No more than 5,200 Jews returned from the concentration camps. And even then, the ones who did, returned traumatized, only to find their family and friends murdered, their possessions stolen, their homes gone.

Members of a Jewish family make their way to the transit camp at Westerbork, 1942.

An eternal flame burns within the memorial chapel at the Hollandsche Schouwburg, where thousands of Jewish men, women, and children awaited their fate.
Opposite: Once again, there is a thriving Jewish community at the heart of Amsterdam's Jodenbuurt district.

The Dutch Schindler

The Dutch had their own Oskar Schindler, in the form of Walter Süskind. A German Jew of Dutch parents, Süskind had been appointed by the Amsterdam Jewish Council in July 1942 to manage the **Hollandsche Schouwburg** (see pp. 91–92), the once opulent theater now being used by the Nazis as a deportation center for Jews. Together with crèche director Henriëtte Pimentel and Amsterdam economist Raphaël "Felix" Halverstad—who also worked at the Hollandsche Schouwburg—Süskind devised a number of plans to make some of these children disappear from the administration, and thus escape.

Duping the Nazi Officers

Having a German mindset and speaking the language fluently, Süskind was able to ingratiate himself with the Nazi officer in charge of deportations. So much so, in fact, that the officer was unaware of the administration being altered to remove any trace of these children. Behind the crèche, children were secretly passed over a wall into the garden of a training college, where women and young girls then smuggled them out in knapsacks, laundry bags, and even milk churns, taking them to safe houses in the Dutch countryside. Sometimes too, children were taken straight out of the front door of the crèche. When a tram pulled up at the stop outside—which is still there to this day—the German guards' view of this heroic activity would be obscured. Süskind would also distract the Germans with jokes or cigars. The children would be bundled onto the tram with the passengers onboard exchanging smiles, since they knew exactly what was going on. Together with Pimentel and Halverstad—and the director of the training college, Johan Wilhelm van Hulst—Süskind is credited with having saved the lives of more than 600 children.

The Fate of the Heroes

Henriëtte Pimentel perished at Aushwitz in 1943. Raphaël Halverstad was on the last transport that left Amsterdam, but managed to escape, and went on to survive the war. And Walter Süskind, himself deported to a concentration camp, is believed to have died on one of the so-called death marches across Europe in February 1945. Today, a plaque at Plantage Middenlaan 31–33 commemorates their bravery, translating as: *In memory of all those who helped rescue Jewish children from deportation during the German occupation. 1940 to 1945.*

Street Markets

Whether you like rummaging around for a one-of-a-kind souvenir, bargaining over a bunch of red tulips, nibbling organic delicacies, or simply soaking up the atmosphere, Amsterdam's street markets are highly browsable affairs. Whatever you do, don't leave town without haggling for a souvenir.

■ Flea Markets

Waterloopleinmarkt (*Waterlooplein, 1011 PG, www. waterlooplein. amsterdam, open 9:30 a.m.–6 p.m.*), named after the square on which it stands in the Jodenbuurt district, is a must-visit. Even though its tourist status means it is a tad overpriced, you'd be hard-pressed to leave empty-handed, thanks to the wide range of wares available here: exotic jewelry, vintage clothes, secondhand books, records, bric-a-brac, and T-shirts galore. Step into some of the shops that surround it, including the organic supermarket **Eko-plaza** (*Waterlooplein 131*) and **Episode** (*Waterlooplein 1*), which sells secondhand and vintage clothes.

■ Art

Spui square, in the Nieuwe Zijde district—flanked at one end by the American Book Center and Waterstones booksellers at the other—is the beating heart of Amsterdam's literary scene. However, every Sunday, from March through December, around 60 contemporary Dutch and international artists sell their work—watercolors, glass objects, jewelry, ceramics, oil paintings, photography, and mixed media—at **Artplein Spui** (*Spui Plein, 1012 WZ, open Sun. 11 a.m.–6 p.m*). While on the square, see if you can spot three pairs of bricks on the ground bearing the words: "A translation from one language to another," written in English, Dutch, Surinamese, and Arabic—the work of New York conceptual artist Lawrence Weiner.

■ Flowers & Plants

Amsterdam's famous floating flower market, **Bloemenmarkt** (*Singel bet. Konigsplein and Muntplein, 1071 AZ,*

JODENBUURT, PLANTAGE, & OOSTERDOK

There are as many as 300 stalls at the world-renowned **Waterlooplein flea market**.

open Mon.–Sat. 9 a.m.–5:30 p.m.; Sun. 11 a.m.–5:30 p.m) is in the Nieuwe Zijde district and needs little introduction (see p. 55). Once you've wandered the length of this daily market, check out the shops opposite for hammocks and other designer goodies. Less touristic—and greener—is the **Bloemen en Plantenmarkt** *(Amstelveld, 1017 JD, open Mon. 9 a.m.–6 p.m.),* which sets up once a week on the picturesque, tree-lined Amstelveld square between Prinsengracht and Keizersgracht in the Southern Canals district.

■ Books

One of Amsterdam's best kept secrets can be found down a tiny covered passageway in the Oude Zijde district. Known as Oudemanhuispoort, it runs between the Oudezijds Achterburgwal and Kloveniersburgwal. Here, the **Oudemanhuispoort Book Market** *(Oudemanhuispoort, 1012 CN, open Mon.–Sat. 11:30 a.m.–6 p.m.)* has been

Leather goods are among the regular finds at Amsterdam's Noodermarkt. It is not unusual to find vendors dealing in cut-rate stock from well-known and designer brands.

in existence for more than two centuries. As early as 1757, stalls were set up within the arches of this historic passage selling books, silver, and gold. Delightfully civilized, quiet, and laid-back, it now specializes in used and antiquarian books, prints, postcards, and sheet music.

■ Clothes & Fabric

If you're after something more special than run-of-the-mill, secondhand clothes, head to the terrific Monday-morning **Noordermarkt** (*1015 MV, open Mon. 9 a.m.–1 p.m. and Sat. 9. a.m.–3 p.m.*), named after the square

it occupies in the Jordaan district (also home to Saturday's organic market; see right). Here you'll find fashionable secondhand clothes and accessories—including some vintage gems—at unbeatable prices. But set your alarm clock: There's stiff competition for the best bargains on offer. Afterward, wander up the **Lapjesmarkt** (*Westerstraat, 1016 DH, open Mon. 9 a.m.–1 p.m.*), a fabric market with sought-after goods that runs from Noordermarkt along Westerstraat.

■ Organic

Amsterdam has two organic markets and both operate on Saturday. The **Boerenmarkt** (*open Sat. 9 a.m.–4 p.m.*) is a farmers market that lies in the shadow of a 17th-century church on Noordermarkt, a small square in the Jordaan district (see left). The Netherlands' first organic market, it has occupied this spot since 1987 and is probably the more charming of the two, with its almost medieval allure. Here you can wander from stall to stall, nibbling on bite-size portions of cheese or sampling wheatgrass juice, as wafts of freshly baked bread perfume the air and buskers provide a gentle background soundtrack. The **Biologische Versmarkt** (*Nieuwmarkt, 1012 CR, open Sat. 9 a.m.–5 p.m.*) is an

A wide range of fresh fruits and vegetables is on sale in the vibrant Albert Cuypmarkt.

organic fresh food market that returns the old town square in the Oude Zijde district to its former 17th-century function as a marketplace. Its more central location means it can get quite busy and you may have to elbow your way to the long cheese stall.

■ General

Amsterdam's largest general market, **Albert Cuypmarkt** (*Albert Cuypstraat, 1072 LL, open Mon.–Sat. 9 a.m.–5 p.m.*), in the de Pijp district, is named after the 17th-century painter Albert Cuyp. Year-round, Monday through Saturday, colorful stalls run almost the entire length of Albert Cuypstraat. Many of them are simply extensions of shops that line the street (these are also worth diving into). This market has a distinctly local feel to it and stallholders tout just about everything, from fresh fish, fruit, and vegetables through footwear, plants, and kitchenware. However, it is the market's reputation for fabrics, not the cheap-looking clothes, that draws hardened bargain-hunters here. Midway up the market, slip into Middle Eastern-style restaurant **Bazar** (*Albert Cuypstraat 182*) for a reviving cup of fresh mint tea.

Northern Canals

The building of Amsterdam's world-famous Grachtengordel—encompassing the Herengracht, Keizersgracht, and Prinsengracht—began in the north of the city during the Dutch Golden Age. It is thanks to this 17th-century canal ring—and its spiderweb of canals that weave around the medieval city—that Amsterdam is sometimes referred to as the Venice of the North. Once the ring was complete, wealthy merchants moved into its elegant houses with *hofjes* (courtyards) concealed behind their facades, and the city expanded rapidly. The district now includes the once working-class, now gentrified, Jordaan and Haarlemmerbuurt districts and the Westelijke Eilanden (Western Islands)—once bustling with tar distillers and fish-salters. In the late 19th-century work began on the Spaarndammerbuurt neighborhood, famous for its Amsterdam School architecture. A certain sense of quiet pervades this district— home to two of the city's most thought- provoking memorials—but there is also a welcome atmosphere of laid-back charm.

108   **Neighborhood Walk**

118   **In Depth:
Anne Frank House**

122   **Distinctly
Amsterdam:
Dutch Courage**

124   **Best Of:
Culinary Delights**

➔ **The terrace of the
Spanjer en van Twist
café on the Leliegracht**

Northern Canals

Enjoy a leisurely stroll through close-knit residential quarters and take time to reflect on the lives of past inhabitants.

⑧ Westergasfabriek Culture Park (see pp. 116–117)
The gentrified gasworks are the perfect place to end your tour. You can choose from several watering holes and eateries, or simply hang out in the park.

⑦ Museum het Schip (see pp. 115–116) This architectural gem is the best place to explore the merits of the Amsterdam School movement, both inside and out. Walk back to the park and head east.

⑥ Westelijk Eilanden (see pp. 114–115) Wander around the Western Islands, then trace your footsteps back to the Haarlemmerplein, and head into the Westerpark. Continue parallel to the railroad line, then turn right into the pedestrian tunnel below it onto the Zaanstraat, and turn left.

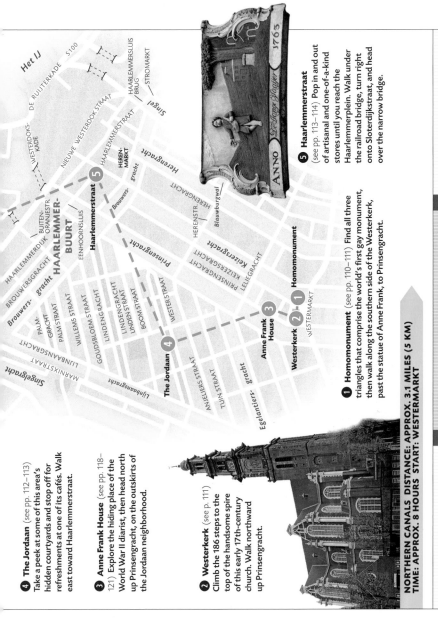

4 The Jordaan (see pp. 112–113)
Take a peek at some of this area's hidden courtyards and stop off for refreshments at one of its cafés. Walk east toward Haarlemmerstraat.

3 Anne Frank House (see pp. 118–121) Explore the hiding place of the World War II diarist, then head north up Prinsengracht, on the outskirts of the Jordaan neighborhood.

2 Westerkerk (see p. 111)
Climb the 186 steps to the top of the handsome spire of this early 17th-century church. Walk northward up Prinsengracht.

5 Haarlemmerstraat
(see pp. 113–114) Pop in and out of artisanal and one-of-a-kind stores untill you reach the Haarlemmerplein. Walk under the railroad bridge, turn right onto Sloterdijkstraat, and head over the narrow bridge.

1 Homomonument (see pp. 110–111) Find all three triangles that comprise the world's first gay monument, then walk along the southern side of the Westerkerk, past the statue of Anne Frank, to Prinsengracht.

NORTHERN CANALS DISTANCE: APPROX. 3.1 MILES (5 KM)
TIME: APPROX. 8 HOURS START: WESTERMARKT

NORTHERN CANALS

Homomonument

1 The progressive Netherlands is home to the world's first gay monument, which was erected below the **Westerkerk** (see opposite) in 1987 to commemorate gay men and women who had been—and continue to be—persecuted because of their sexuality; it also serves as a reminder that Jews were not the only victims of Nazi concentration camps. Designed by Karin Daan, it consists of three pink-granite triangles—one raised, one flush with the ground, and one that steps down into the Keizersgracht canal. Together, they make a larger triangle, where the orientation of each corner has great significance: One points to **Anne Frank House** (see pp. 118–121), another to the **Nationaal Monument** in **Dam Square** (see p. 50), and the last to headquarters of the Dutch gay rights organization. On World AIDS Day (Dec. 1) and other notable days—Remembrance Day (May 4), Liberation Day (May 5), King's Day (April 27), and, of course, the annual Gay Pride (July/August)—it becomes the

Wreaths and flowers appear regularly on the Homomonument steps, often with messages.

focal point of the city's thriving gay community. Beer tents and music stages are set up, and locals and visitors dance on the triangles and enjoy the so-called Drag Queen Olympics. For a souvenir, or for more information, pop into the **Pink Point,** a little kiosk in the square that is open year-round.

Westermarkt, 1016 DJ • www.homomonument.nl • Tram: 13, 17

Westerkerk

2 Designed by architect Hendrick de Keyser, the Dutch Renaissance-style Western Church was built between 1620 and 1631; its 275-foot-high (84 m) spire—the highest in Amsterdam—was completed in 1638. Look up and you'll see the blue Imperial Crown of Austria. In 1489, the Holy Roman Emperor, Maximilian I, gave the city permission to incorporate the crown in its coat of arms. At the time, it was a hugely important gesture for Amsterdam, serving as a hallmark of trustworthiness, similar to the way in which, in Great Britain, a royal warrant endorses a product or service. During the summer months, you can climb up to the first floor of the tower, where you'll be rewarded with great views and a display offering a brief history of the church. Rembrandt is buried here, in an unmarked pauper's grave. When bankruptcy forced the artist to leave his home in Jodenbreestraat (see pp. 96–97), he lived in this district from 1658 until his death in 1669. Nothing remains of his house today, but a plaque at **Rozengracht 184** marks the spot. Anne Frank went into hiding practically next door to the Westerkerk and mentioned the carillon in her diary. She found its quarter-hourly chimes reassuring. Don't miss Marie Andriessen's statue of Anne Frank, erected in 1977 on the southern side of the church.

Prinsengracht 281, 1016 GW • www.westerkerk.nl • 020 624 7766 • Closed Sat. and Sun. • Tram: 13, 17

NORTHERN CANALS

NORTHERN CANALS

Anne Frank House

3 See pp. 118–121.

Westermarkt 20, 1016 GV • www.annefrank.org • 020 556 7105 • €
• Closed: Yom Kippur • Tram: 13, 17

The Jordaan

4 The Jordaan is a small residential area sandwiched between Prinsengracht and Lijnbaansgracht, with Brouwersgracht to the north and Leidsegracht to the south. There are several theories as to why this area is named the Jordaan, the most plausible being that it's a corruption of the French word *jardin*. The district's original, 17th-century inhabitants were French-speaking religious refugees who referred to it as "the garden," and many of its streets are named after flowers or plants: Palmstraat (Palm Street) and Goudsbloemstraat (Marigold Street), for example. Once inhabited by the working

A cool, relaxed atmosphere pervades the narrow, often maze-like streets of the Jordaan district.

classes, the streets are now scattered with upscale boutiques and designer stores, with enough cafés and bars to make shopping a relaxing experience.

This quiet area is dotted with a number of surprises, so keep your eyes peeled for various gable stones and odd sculptural features on the buildings. The area is especially renowned for its *hofjes*—hidden courtyards traditionally built for impoverished elderly widows. Stroll up the road from the **Anne Frank House** to Zon's Hofje *(Prinsengracht 159–171)*, push open the gate, and take a peek inside. Then walk a few doors up to view the beautifully manicured garden of the larger Van Brienenhofje *(Prinsengracht 85–153)*, dating from 1804, once the site of a brewery.

Metro: Centraal Station • Tram: 5, 13, 17, 19

Haarlemmerstraat

5 Haarlemmerdijk—the old road that led from Amsterdam to the neighboring town of Haarlem—is the main thoroughfare of another recently gentrified area of the city, Haarlemmerbuurt, just north of the Jordaan. Running northwest to southeast, Haarlemmerdijk turns into Haarlemmerstraat, before snaking round into the **Nieuwe Zijde's** pedestrianized shopping street, Nieuwendijk. While its Nieuwe Zijde counterpart is filled with commercial shops and chains, this strip is geared more toward artisanal and specialty stores. Walking east toward **Centraal Station** (see p. 48), you'll discover the **West-Indisch Huis** (see p. 30), former headquarters of the Dutch West India company. Across the road is the **Posthoornkerk** *(Haarlemmerstraat 124–126)*, a striking three-spired church dating from 1860 and designed by the man behind the **Rijksmuseum** (see pp. 158–161) and Centraal Station, P. J. H. Cuypers. Nowadays, it's used only for private events and occasional

GOOD **EATS**

■ **SMALL WORLD**
Soup, sandwiches, pasta dishes, and imaginative salads; fresh juices, scones, muffins, brownies, and a carrot cake to die for! Eat in or takeout. **Binnen Oranjestraat 14, 1013 JA, 020 420 2774, €**

■ **SONNEVELD**
This café, located exactly in front of the Westerkerk and dedicated to the artist, Wim Sonneveld, offers breakfast, lunch, and dinner, 365 days a year. **Egelantiersgracht 72–74, 1015 RM, 020 423 4287, €€**

■ **WINKEL 43**
Enjoy a slice of the best apple pie in town on peaceful Noordermarkt square. **Noordermarkt 43, 1015 NA, 020 623 0223, €**

NORTHERN CANALS

exhibitions. Walk west toward Haarlemmerplein and the Singelgracht canal and you'll find the **Haarlemmerpoort,** built in 1840. When 20th-century city planners decided to build a busy road around this neoclassical arch, complete with tram lines, it became somewhat obsolete. En route, don't miss one of the area's absolute gems—**The Movies** (*Haarlemmerdijk 159–163*)—an art deco cinema dating from 1912 within a very narrow, 17th-century building. If it's raining, why not pop in here and catch a recently released independent film or Hollywood blockbuster?

Metro: Centraal Station • Tram: 3

Westelijk Eilanden

The Western Islands comprise three man-made islands— **Bickerseiland, Prinseneiland,** and **Realeneiland.** Created between 1611 and 1615, they formed part of the city ramparts along

the IJ River. Back then the area was brimming with shipping wharves and warehouses, piled high with herring, grain, tobacco, wine, salt, anchovies, and even cat skins. Today, the area is one of the city's most sought-after, residentially—inhabited mostly by artists, actors, and musicians—and it's not hard to see why: its tall gentrified warehouses, its small wooden bridges, and its characterful canals with colorful houseboats. At **Prinseneiland 24B** you'll find an atelier constructed in 1898 by George Hendrik Breitner. He was a painter and photographer, who often worked with Vincent van Gogh and whose work can be seen in the Rijksmuseum; he worked here until 1914. There are few sites, but many charming corners to explore. Simply walk from island to island enjoying the peace and quiet and when you are tired, park your weary feet on the terrace of the **Gouden Reael** (*Zandhoek 14)* and enjoy the view. This historic bar-restaurant

Handsome, multistory warehouses line the streets of the Westelijk Eilanden— testimony to Amsterdam's rich trading history.

NORTHERN CANALS

was once a herring warehouse. Just over 150 years ago the building became an inn and was where the harbor workers would relax with a beer or jenever (see pp. 122–123).

Metro: Centraal Station • Tram: 3

Museum het Schip

⑦ This rather unconventional looking building, nicknamed The Ship, is a classic example of the Amsterdam School architectural movement (ca 1910–1930). Many consider the style to be the Dutch version of art deco, although it went much further than that. Central to the movement was the belief that art should be for everyone, regardless of class. The Ship was designed in 1919 by Michel de Klerk and, for many, it represents the pinnacle of Dutch social housing. The building houses 120 homes for working-class families, a small meeting hall, and a post office. With its orange bricks, undulating walls, distinctive windows, and richly decorated works of art, it was dubbed a workers' palace. As de Klerk himself put it: "Nothing is too good for the worker who has had to do without beauty for so very long."

A number of white, wooden drawbridges span the canals of the Westelijk Eilanden, raised in past times to allow tall cargo ships into the docks.

Still largely inhabited by families on lower incomes the building now has a **Museum Residence,** where you can visit an apartment restored to its original 1920s incarnation—right down to the utensils. A second apartment functions as an exhibition space offering details on de Klerk and this unique architectural movement. To get the most out of your visit take a free tour given in English by enthusiastic volunteers: There's one every hour. The 3 p.m. tour is always in English but if you contact the museum, it's possible to have a tour in English at other times, as well. The pièce de resistance is probably the **post office**—the last interior de Klerk ever designed—which, from the outside, looks like the funnel of a ship. Look at the details

NORTHERN CANALS

An icon of its time, the beautifully tiled phone booth in the post office at Museum Het Schip

the architect added to the telephone booth: The bars on the windows resemble telegraph wires and, if you look closely, you'll see birds perched on them. Notice, too, the door to what was once the mail sorting area, marked *verboden* (forbidden). Because many of the working-class residents couldn't read, it has a hand holding a truncheon carved into it.

Spaarndammerplantsoen 140, 1013 XT • www. hetschip.nl • 020 686 8595 • €€ • Closed Mon., Jan. 1, King's Day, and Dec. 25 • Tram: 3

Westergasfabriek Culture Park

8 The now-defunct Western Gasworks was constructed at the end of the 19th century. Having originally supplied the city's streetlights, today it serves as an extraordinary creative hub. Not only are its grounds, including an enormous gas holder, used for festivals, concerts, cultural events, and parties, but entrepreneurs, artists, fashion designers, filmmakers, and chocolate artisans rent workshops and retail spaces in the various buildings, many of which are open to the public. Also on site is the **Ketelhuis,** a cinema dedicated to the Dutch film industry. Do check the listings, as films are often subtitled in English.

Highlights here are undoubtedly the cafés and restaurants. Walk across the iron bridge by the main entrance and wafts of scones and baked bread will signal the **Bakkerswinkel** (*Polonceaukade 1 and 2*). Walk a little farther, past the Ketelhuis, and you'll discover the award-winning **Espressofabriek** (*Pazzanistraat 39*), purveyors of the finest espresso—and all its variations—in town. Beyond is **Pacific Amsterdam** (*Polonceaukade 23*), an enormous, high-ceilinged café-restaurant with a large, chilled terrace. On weekend nights DJs spin and it turns into a noisy, crowded club. For some of the tastiest food in town walk beyond Pacific Amsterdam to **Raïnaraï** *(Polonceaukade 40),* where you can enjoy Algerian food in an authentic interior.

Allow time to stroll through the park, which was designed by American landscape artist Kathyrn Gustafson, responsible for the Diana Memorial Fountain in London's Hyde Park. In sunny weather, the locals come here to play tennis, enjoy picnics, and read books. Walk to the farthest western point and you'll find a **Children's Farm** *(www.boerderijwesterpark.nl)* with ponies, a cow, a pig, sheep, goats, and rabbits. It's no surprise that with all it has to offer, the Westergasfabriek Culture Park won a European Heritage Award in 2010.

Haarlemmerweg 8–10, 1014 BE • www.westergasfabriek.nl • Tram: 5

One of the many food trucks at the annual (May) Rolling Kitchens Festival at Westergasfabriek Culture Park, a food festival on wheels

Anne Frank House

A visit to the hiding place of this wartime diarist brings the Jewish teenager's compelling words to life.

Otto Frank's employee, Mr. Kugler, constructed a bookcase to conceal the entrance to the annex.

Annelies Marie Frank—better known as Anne Frank—needs little introduction. Her diary has been translated into more than 70 languages and is one of the most widely read books in the world. The hiding place of this young Jewish woman, her father Otto, mother Edith, sister Margot, and four other family friends during the Nazi occupation of World War II is one of the city's most popular sights. And a visit to its confined, clandestine rooms—accessed by a movable bookcase—counts as one of life's more sobering experiences.

Exhibition Space

The museum occupies two houses on Prinsengracht on the edge of the Jordaan area (see pp. 112–113)—the house in which Anne Frank, her family, and family friends hid (No. 263), and its neighbor (No. 265). The latter serves as the museum entrance and an exhibition space today. Here, a permanent collection dedicated to Anne Frank's life story is supplemented by temporary exhibitions, which have included photographs and letters, and the stories of other family members.

Anne's Diary

It is in the exhibition space that you can see pages from Anne's original green-and-red-checked diary, a gift from her father on June 12, 1942. Within three weeks of receiving the diary, Anne and her family had gone into hiding in the *achterhuis* (see p. 120). While living there, Anne penned her personal thoughts and experiences in the diary to an imaginary friend she called Kitty. She wrote about life in the annex, changing the names of the people she was living with: Family friends, the Van Pels family—Hermann, August, and their son Peter—became the Van Daans, while dentist Fritz Pfeffer was

SAVVY **TRAVELER**

With more than one million visitors a year, Anne Frank House is one of the three most popular museums in Amsterdam. To avoid the worst of the lines, buy your tickets in advance online or visit toward the end of the day. To see how the annex looked during the war, join a virtual tour of the annex online. If you have a pair of VR glasses, you can use a special app to explore the rooms. Each of the rooms is furnished as it would have been in 1944, based on the model reconstructions that Otto commissioned for the museum in 1961.

known as Mr. Dussel. Anne wrote her final entry on August 1, 1944. Three days after that, she was betrayed and arrested with her family and the other inhabitants of the annex and deported. When Otto Frank returned to Amsterdam after the war—the only surviving member of the annex—Miep Gies, who had helped the family when they were in hiding, handed Anne's diary to the grief-stricken Otto.

Living in Secrecy

From the exhibition space, you can enter the rooms at the front of the house at **Prinsengracht 263**—former offices of Otto Frank's business. Walking through reconstructions of the rooms as they were in the 1940s, you can imagine how difficult it must have been for the business to run as usual. Only a handful of employees knew of the existence of the family in hiding, all too aware that their discovery would have tragic consequences. Yet it was thanks to the few who did know—the helpers—that the Franks and their cohabitants were able to live in total secrecy for more than two years before finally being betrayed to the Nazis. Later, when the house was opened to the public in 1960, it was also these helpers who led the first public tours of the secret annex.

■ A Tour of Anne's Annex

The undoubted highlight of the museum is a visit to the *achterhuis*—the annex that adjoins Prinsengracht 263 to the rear. Walk in via the movable bookcase on the second floor of the house, a copy of the original. You'd think the tour would be a test of your imagination, because the rooms remain as Otto found them

Peter Van Pel slept in a makeshift room on the landing at the foot of the attic stairs.

on his return to Amsterdam after the war and are almost completely empty. Following the family's discovery, all the furniture and other items were removed—and thereafter stolen or sold—as was typical when Jews were deported.

Once inside, however, it is not difficult to grasp how life must have been in such confinement. For immediately behind the bookcase is a small hallway and the door to the Franks' living quarters: one room that Anne's sister and parents slept in; and a second room that Anne had to share with the dentist, Fritz Pfeffer. Today a few photographs and pictures that Anne cut from newspapers remain pasted to the walls, but there is little more. At one end of the room is the sole bathroom, woefully ill-equipped with just a washbasin and a toilet that could only be flushed at night, once the workers from the warehouse on the floor below had gone home.

Exit the bathroom to return to the hallway where you can climb the stairs to the Van Pels' living quarters—for the most part a large room in which Mr. and Mrs. Van Pel

A photo of Anne smiling without a care in the world, the year before going into hiding

slept, but that also served as the communal kitchen, dining room, and living room. Pass through the narrow door to the right of where the kitchen once stood, and you'll be standing in Peter Van Pel's room—nothing more than the landing at the bottom of the stairs to the attic. Complete the tour by ascending the steep stairs to the attic and—as Anne did on several occasions—take a few moments in privacy to reflect on her life.

Westermarkt 20, 1016 GV • www.annefrank.org • 020 556 7105 • € • Closed Yom Kippur • Tram: 13, 17

NORTHERN CANALS

Dutch Courage

If you had to think of a drink that was typically Dutch, it would be Heineken. Thanks to some shrewd advertising, brewery acquisitions, and international trading—which the Dutch do so well—Heineken is one of the world's most ubiquitous beer brands. And it all started in Amsterdam. But don't leave town without tasting the wares of the city's smaller breweries—along with jenever, the venerable forerunner of gin.

NORTHERN CANALS

The Dutch are particularly known for their pale lagers, Heineken and Grolsch, but also produce darker, more bitter beers in some regions. The Netherlands also has one Trappist brewery, De Koningshoeven.

Here for the Beer?

Three major beers are brewed in the Netherlands. Amstel (first brewed in 1870 and named after the river) and Heineken (first brewed in 1873) originated in Amsterdam. A third beer, Grolsch, dates back to 1615 and originated in the town of Grolle (now known as Groenlo), in the east of the country. The Dutch also produce *witbier* (white beer), a light-colored, sweet-tasting beer. All are served with two fingers of froth, said to enhance the taste in the way that the *crema* layer of an espresso does.

The Origin of Jenever

Jenever was first made in the Middle Ages by Sylvius de Bouve, a professor and chemist at Leiden University. He added juniper berries—believed to have medicinal benefits—to distilled alcohol. And by 1595, he was selling his healthful tipple as a remedy for lower back pain under the name Genova. By the end of the 17th century, the Dutch were exporting more than 10 million gallons (45 million liters) of this medicinal spirit, jenever distilleries were all the rage, and *proeflokalen* (tasting rooms) had popped up all over Amsterdam. A few remain to this day and serve a variety of flavored jenevers, including the highly flavorsome Bessen Jenever (berry jenever). These establishments usually open mid-afternoon and close around 8 p.m. Roughly speaking, jenever is categorized by its age: *jong* (young), *oud* (old), and *zeer oud* (very old)—the older, the smoother. An old jenever contains more malt-based alcohol, while a young jenever uses new distilling techniques and contains more grain-based alchohol. Finally, a *kopstoot* (blow on the head) is drinking a jenever in combination with a pilsner. Another Dutch tradition. Cheers! Or as they say in the Netherlands: *Proost!*

DON'T **MISS**

Wynand Fockink (*www. wynand-fockink.nl*), down a little passageway off Dam Square at Pijlsteeg 31, is Amsterdam's most charming *proeflokaal*. Founded in 1679, it sells old Dutch liquors and jenevers, some of which are produced on the premises. The drinks menu is a delight: Naked Belly Button (made for moms-to-be); Bridal Tears (traditionally served after marriage ceremonies when the city hall was located on Dam Square); and Lotion of Venus with its reputed aphrodisiac powers.

Serving jenever at De Drie Fleschjes (The Three Little Bottles) *proeflokaal* **in Amsterdam**

Culinary Delights

The Dutch are not particularly renowned for their prowess in the kitchen. Instead, traditional Dutch food is rather basic, simple "farmers' fare" used for filling up or warming up. Thankfully, however, there are a number of Dutch delights worth seeking out on your visit to Amsterdam.

■ Pannenkoeken

No trip to Amsterdam would be complete without partaking in a pancake or two. But don't play safe: Try one with cheese, ham, and . . . *stroop* (syrup). It's an odd combination but surprisingly

The oldest known Dutch recipe for apple pie comes from an early 16th-century cookbook.

delicious. Most Amsterdam cafés serve them, but the best place to indulge in them is in the dedicated **Pancake Bakery** (*Prinsengracht 191, 020 625 1333, €*), housed in a 17th-century VOC warehouse and just up the road from the **Anne Frank House** (see pp. 118–121). *Poffertjes*, a smaller, puffier variety of pancake—served fresh, warm, and sprinkled with powdered sugar—are also scrumptious.

■ Appeltart

Apple pie is not exclusive to the Dutch by any means, but it is something they do very well and have been doing so for centuries. Most cafés serve it—usually with a generous dollop of whipped cream—but for the perfect cinnamon-infused creation, you should head to **Winkel 43** (*Noordermarkt 43, 020 623 0223, €*), located on the corner of Noordermarkt and Westerstraat in the Jordaan district.

NORTHERN CANALS

Rijsttafel

Rice table. A tour de force of Dutch cuisine that comes all the way from Indonesia. Between 1800 and 1945, the Southeast Asian archipelago was a Dutch colony and the Dutch devised this meal—or feast, in fact—consisting of a multitude of spicy side dishes served with rice. Try the authentic **Tempo Doeloe** (*Utrechtsestraat 75, 020 625 6718, €€€*) in the Nieuwe Zijde district or the more modern **Kantijl & De Tijger** (*Spuistraat 291–293, 020 620 0994, €€€*) in the Jodenbuurt district.

Drop

The Dutch eat more licorice per capita than any other nation in the world! It comes in all shapes and sizes, but there are basically two different types: *zoet* (sweet) and *zout* (salty). Not only is it tasty, it's also great for sore throats. For a great selection head to **Jacob Hooy & Co.** (see pp. 69–70) in the Oude Zijde district, an 18th-century herb and spices shop turned 21st-century pharmacy.

Erwtensoep

This extremely thick pea soup is very delicious. Also known as *snert,* it's traditionally eaten during winter, served with rye bread topped with bacon. The test of the best is if your spoon can stand upright in it. You can order *erwtensoep*

SAVVY **TRAVELER**

Dotted around town, **Febo** is a chain of fast-food outlets with a difference. Imagine a wall of coin-operated vending machines that work a bit like ATMs—but instead of cash, you get hamburgers, croquettes, and french fries with mayonnaise or curry sauce (a Dutch phenomenon). Although pretty much devoid of nutrition, it has to be said that gratification is immediate and the food is cheap (a couple of euros at most.)

and other authentic Dutch dishes, such as *hutspot* and *bitterballen* (see below and p. 126), at **The Pantry** (*Leidsekruisstraat 21, 020 620 0922, €–€€*) in the Southern Canals district.

Hutspot

Legend has it that the recipe for *hutspot*—hotchpotch, or shaken pot—came from a dish left by fleeing Spanish soldiers when the city of Leiden was liberated from its 1574 siege during the Eighty Years' War. Basic ingredients are mashed potatoes, carrots, and onions. *Stamppot* (mash pot) is a variation that includes *rookworst* (smoked sausage) or *spek* (bacon), and often *boerenkool* (farmers' cabbage or kale). These hearty dishes, served at The Pantry (see above), are supremely warming during Amsterdam's chilly winters.

Wall-to-wall cheese at De Kaaskamer in the Nine Streets area of the Southern Canals district

■ Bitterballen

These deep-fried meatballs (not bitter at all, they simply take their name from bitter beer) are a ubiquitous Dutch snack, usually served with alcoholic drinks as a savory stomach-filler. You'll find them in almost any brown café (see p. 81) in the city. Be careful when tasting them as they can be piping hot inside.

■ Kaas

It's no surprise that the Dutch are known as cheeseheads. They consume a whopping 48 pounds (22 kg) of the stuff on average each year. In fact, many will usually have a cheese sandwich washed down with a glass of milk for lunch.

Edam and Gouda are probably the most famous cheeses—and both are named after towns in the Netherlands. But a trip to **De Kaaskamer** (*Runstraat 7, 020 623 3483*) in the Southern Canals district, a shop devoted entirely to cheese, will prove to be an enlightening experience. Pop in to sample their baguette of the week. Otherwise, keep an eye out for free cheese samples at organic food and farmers markets.

■ Stroopwafel

The recipe for this caramel-like, syrup-filled cookie originates from the city of Gouda, also renowned for its famous cheese. You'll find freshly made *stroopwafel* at **Albert Cuypmarkt** (see

p. 156) in the Pijp district—the more handmade the variety, the more mouthwatering they are. Other cookie goodness comes in the form of the *speculaas,* a crisp, spiced cookie flavored with pepper, cinnamon, ginger, cloves, cardamom, and nutmeg. Once only baked around Sinterklaas (Saint Nicholas) feast at the beginning of December, these days supermarkets—and duty-free shops—stock them by the tin load.

■ Oliebollen

These deep-fried doughnuts are stodgy dough balls—usually containing raisins and apples and sprinkled with sticky confectioner's sugar—that are traditionally eaten on New Year's Eve. However, most bakeries serve them throughout the wintertime, and they can also be found at fairgrounds or at street stalls. The Dutch have been eating these morsels for centuries and for that reason alone, they're worth tasting.

■ Haring

The Dutch love their fish. Especially herring—which they commonly pickle in brine and sell as street food. Keep your eye out for stalls serving it with chopped raw onions and pickled cucumber; throw your head back, slip it in, and take a bite!

Hollandse Nieuwe—Dutch for the first herring of the season—with pickled cucumber and onions

Southern Canals

This southern section of the iconic Grachtengordel (Canal Ring) was constructed in the 17th century, during Amsterdam's Golden Age. Herengracht, Keizersgracht, and Prinsengracht radiate from the city's medieval center in concentric fashion, rather like a spiderweb. Their names—Patrician's Canal, Emperor's Canal, and Prince's Canal—reflect the prosperity of the age, as do the facades of the prestigious houses that line them. Short, narrow, radial canals were added to provide links from one canal ring to the next. Many of these radial canals were filled in around the turn of the 20th century, but picturesque Leidsegracht and Reguliersgracht survive. Among the many pleasures in this district are the canals themselves and a handful of canalside houses that are now open to the public as museums. This is also great territory for shopping, whether seeking fine art or antiques in the Spiegelkwartier, or browsing the many independent stores that fill the quaint streets of De Negen Straatjes area.

130 **Neighborhood Walk**

140 **In Depth:
     Museum van Loon**

142 **Distinctly
     Amsterdam: Tulips**

144 **Best Of:
     Canals**

**◐ Originally a moat,
the Singel is the
innermost of the
concentric canals
that surround
Amsterdam's
medieval center.**

SOUTHERN CANALS

⑩ Woonbootmuseum (see p. 139) **Finish up on this old barge, now the Houseboat Museum, to learn all about life on Amsterdam's canals.**

⑨ De Negen Straatjes (see pp. 138–139) **Treat yourself to some boutique purchases in this grid of nine narrow shopping streets. Make your way to Prinsengracht, just south of Berenstraat.**

⑧ Kattenkabinet (see pp. 137–138) **Step into Herengracht 497 for a tour of the rooms on the second floor, which house a museum dedicated to cats. Head north along Herengracht.**

❼ Spiegelkwartier (see p. 136) **See what art, antiques, and objets d'art take your fancy as you stroll between the canals along the Nieuwe Spiegelstraat and Kerkstraat. Follow Nieuwe Spiegelstraat until you reach Herengracht.**

❻ Museum van Loon (see pp. 140–141) **Tour the elegant home of one of Amsterdam's influential merchant families. Head south down Vijzelstraat and turn right onto Kerkstraat.**

**SOUTHERN CANALS DISTANCE: APPROX. 3 MILES (5 KM)
TIME: APPROX. 8 HOURS START: KERKSTRAAT/AMSTEL RIVER**

Southern Canals

Lavish interiors, quirky museums, and deluxe shopping lie in store as you zigzag the Herengracht, Keizersgracht, and Prinsengracht canals.

❶ Magere Brug (see p. 132) One of Amsterdam's most iconic bridges, the wooden Magere Brug provides a fun start to exploring the Southern Canals district. From Kerkstraat, cross over the bridge and head north along the Amstel.

❷ Hermitage Amsterdam (see pp. 132–134) From Russia with love: Admire rich pickings selected from the three million exhibits held by Russia's Hermitage Museum in St. Petersburg. Continue north and cross the bridge at Waterlooplein.

❸ Museum Willet-Holthuysen (see p. 134) Walk along the west bank of the Amstel River and then into Herengracht to see how the other half lived at this exceptional canalside house (no. 605). Afterward, continue up Herengracht.

AMSTEL

Amstel

EMBRANDT-PLEIN

HORBECKE-LEIN

Museum Willet-Holthuysen

❸

AMSTEL

NIEUWE HERENGRACHT

NIEUWE KEIZERSGRACHT

Hermitage Amsterdam

❷

Nieuwe Keizersgracht

NIEUWE KEIZERSGRACHT

❹

Reguliersgracht

KEIZERSGRACHT

AMSTEL

NIEUWE KERKSTRAAT

REGULIERSGRACHT

KERKSTRAAT

UTRECHTSE STRAAT

PRINSENGRACHT

❶

Magere Brug

NIEUWE PRINSENGRACHT

Nieuwe Prinsengracht

WEESPER STRAAT

AMSTEL-VELD

PRINSENGRACHT

ACHTER-GRACHT

Amstel-sluizen

REGULIERSGRACHT

FALCK-STRAAT

FREDERIKS-PLEIN

❹ Reguliersgracht (see p. 135) Stop to count the famous Seven Bridges along this narrow canal. Head into Reguliersgracht and turn right along Keizersgracht.

❺ Foam Museum (see p. 135) Check out the current exhibitions at this handsome canalside house turned photography museum. Cross the bridge at Vijzelstraat to the other side of the canal.

SOUTHERN CANALS

View of the Magere Brug

Magere Brug

1 Spanning the Amstel River at Kerkstraat, the Skinny Bridge is an entirely wooden structure with access limited to cyclists and pedestrians. It is of bascule design, which means it can open in the middle to allow large vessels to pass through (an event that happens several times a day). Its name derives from the first of three structures to cross the Amstel River in this location, two of which have long since perished. The story goes that two sisters who lived on opposite sides of the river had the bridge built in 1691, in order to speed up their visits to each other. A lack of funding resulted in a precariously narrow bridge. It became known locally as the skinny bridge and the name has stuck ever since.

Amstel 81, 1018 EK • Metro: Waterlooplein • Tram: 4

Hermitage Amsterdam

2 Hermitage Amsterdam occupies the former Amstelhof, a large building with a long, classical facade constructed in 1681 to house the elderly. There are three permanent presentations here: The Portrait Gallery of the 17th Century, in collaboration with the Rijksmuseum, offers the public a view of thirty very large portraits, which, precisely because of their size, are rarely displayed. The "brothers and sisters" (as the museums call them) of Rembrandt's

"The Night Watch" represent the collective population, giving a face to merchants, scholars, and religious figures of every social class; the Outsider Art, in collaboration with the museum of the same name, is unusual and decidedly "outside the box" as its name suggests; and Panorama Amsterdam. City Time Lapse uses projection technology to chronicle the development of the city, from the Middle Ages to the present, with the Hermitage building as the presentation's vantage point. The undoubted highlight, however, is the museum's outstanding program of temporary exhibitions, which draws on the enormous collections of the Hermitage Museum in St. Petersburg, Russia. Past shows include rich displays of life in imperial Russia, as well as features on the works of Flemish masters and the French Impressionists and Postimpressionists, for example. Check the museum website to see

Most of the temporary exhibitions at Hermitage Amsterdam enjoy a six-month run.

Rococo-style furnishings exude style and luxury at Museum Willet-Holthuysen.

SOUTHERN CANALS

what's on during your visit. Hermitage Amsterdam has a special children's section housed in the adjacent **Neerlandia Building,** but almost all of the activities are in Dutch.

Amstel 51, 1018 EJ • www.hermitage.nl • 020 530 8758 • €€€ • Closed King's Day and Dec. 25 • Metro: Waterlooplein • Tram: 14

Museum Willet-Holthuysen

3 Three floors of this former private house on the north side of **Herengracht** are open to the public and provide a glimpse of the opulent living quarters of members of Amsterdam's 19th-century elite. Built in around 1685 for Jacob Hop, the mayor of Amsterdam, the house was bought by the Willet-Holthuysen family in 1850. Abraham Willet was a wealthy art collector and bon vivant from an affluent Amsterdam family; much of his collection hangs in the house. His wife, Louisa Holthuysen, furnished the house in the style of Louis XVI, with its typical mix of rococo and neoclassical elements. In 1889 she bequeathed the house and its contents to the city. The entrance is on the lower-ground floor, where you can see the kitchen. The **Blue Room,** on the ground floor, has intense indigo-colored walls. Upstairs, on the first floor, a small red salon with stained-glass windows looks out over the neat, French-style garden, which you can reach via the lower-ground floor.

Herengracht 605, 1001 AC • www.willetholthuysen.nl • 020 523 1822 • €€ • Metro: Waterlooplein • Tram: 4, 14

Reguliersgracht

4 Reguliersgracht is one of the surviving "radial" canals in this part of the city—rescued from developers at the turn of the 20th century. If you stand on the bridge at the junction of Reguliersgracht with **Herengracht,** and look south along the canal, you will see a series of arched bridges. Chances are you won't be able to distinguish them all as they merge in the distance, but there are seven altogether—the bridge on which you're standing, two bridges at **Keizersgracht,** one at **Kerkstraat,** two at **Prinsengracht,** and one out at **Lijnbaansgracht.**

Herengracht 536 • Metro: Waterlooplein • Tram: 4, 14

Foam Museum

5 The Foam Museum on Keizersgracht is actually more of a series of galleries, and features three different exhibitions on its four floors at any one time. While promoting up-and-coming talent, the museum also hosts the work of four world-famous photographers each year. In the past, these have included retrospectives of the work of Magnum founder, Henri Cartier-Bresson, and the celebrated fashion and portrait photographer Richard Avedon. The museum is also worth visiting from an architectural standpoint, if only to see the different kinds of modern space that can be created within a 17th-century house. With its large and small rooms, glass gangways, and spiral staircases, this is an arresting example of contemporary gallery design. On the opposite side of Keizersgracht is the **Museum van Loon.**

Keizersgracht 609, 1017 DS • www.foam.org • 020 551 6500 • € • Closed King's Day • Tram: 2, 4, 9, 11, 12, 14, 24

IN **THE KNOW**

Roof gables are an integral part of Amsterdam's charm, and as you walk around the Southern Canals you'll see that they're not all the same. The three basic types are easy to identify once you know their names: the 17th-century stepped gable, the neck gable (1640–1780), and the bell gable (1660–1790). The last two often have elaborate sculptural decorations on their edges and crest, to help conceal the roofline behind. If built during the classicism period from the mid- to late 17th century, they might also be topped with a rounded or triangular pediment.

SOUTHERN CANALS

Museum van Loon

6 See pp. 140–141.

Keizersgracht 672, 1017 ET • www.museumvanloon.nl • 020 624 5255 • €
• Closed Jan. 1, King's Day, and Dec. 25 • Metro: Vijzelgracht • Tram: 24

Spiegelkwartier

7 The Mirror Quarter stretches from **Spiegelgracht,** along **Nieuwe Spiegelstraat,** and all the way through to **Herengracht.** This is Amsterdam's principal art and antiques district, with more than 80 shops dealing in pictures, furniture, glass, and ceramics. They include **Meulendijks & Schuil** (*Nieuwe Spiegelstraat 45A*), one of the city's most fascinating shops, crammed with clocks, globes, navigational aids, model trains, traction engines, games, telescopes and binoculars, beautiful model ships, and, most astonishingly, large-scale models of biplanes and monoplanes hanging from the ceiling! Among the shops specializing in antique furniture and Delftware are **Aronson Antiquairs** (*Nieuwe Spiegelstraat 45*) and **Kramer Kunst & Antiek** (*Prinsengracht 807*). For those with an interest in art, **Salomon Lilian** (*Spiegelgracht 5*) deals in 17th-century Dutch and Flemish paintings.

As well as selling vintage blue-and-white Delftware, Kramer Kunst & Antiek specializes in antique tiles from around the world.

Nieuwe Spiegelstraat, 1017 DC • Tram: 1, 2, 5

The Kattenkabinet is situated on the second floor of a grand house. The elegant rooms have many period features including, in this former ballroom, paneled walls.

Kattenkabinet

8 This eccentric museum of all things feline was created in honor of the owner's pet cat and companion for almost twenty years. An extraordinary collection of posters, sculptures, drawings, and paintings, the Cat Museum contains works of art by Picasso, Rembrandt, and Toulouse-Lautrec, among others. A visit to this museum also gives you the chance to take a look inside one of the magnificent canalside houses that line the **Gouden Bocht** (Golden Bend), a curve of the Herengracht between Vijzelstraat and Leidsestraat, where Nieuwe Spiegelstraat meets the canal. Taking in the broad sweep of magnificent facades, you'll see that these are no longer mere town houses, but double-fronted mansions, their neoclassical facades making them less typically Amsterdam than the smaller, older houses of the 17th century with their distinctive gables.

Nowadays, if not privately occupied, most of these houses are given over to banks, insurance companies, and consulates.

Herengracht 497, 1017 BT • www.kattenkabinet.nl • 020 626 9040 • € • Closed Jan. 1, King's Day, and Dec. 25, 26, 31 • Tram: 1, 2, 5, 25

De Negen Straatjes

9 It is fun to roam and browse De Negen Straatjes, nine narrow streets positioned at right angles to the main canals between Leidsegracht and Westermarkt. From south to north the first streets are Wijde Heisteeg, Huidenstraat, and Runstraat; then come Oude Spiegelstraat, Wolvenstraat, and Berenstraat; followed by Gasthuismolensteeg, Hartenstraat, and Reestraat. The streets are known for their variety of small independent shops. Natural soaps are the attraction at **La Savonnerie** (*Prinsengracht 294*). They're available in more than seventy different scents (and in unscented versions for those with very sensitive skin),

Fans of vintage clothing try on 1970s floppy hats at Laura Dols.

in addition to other products from the same line, including towels and baskets. **Laura Dols Vintage Clothing** (*Wolvenstraat 7*) is the most famous vintage store in Amsterdam and sells a range of dresses and outfits, shoes, and clutches from various decades (with a special focus on the Fifties). **Pontifex** (*Reestraat 20*) is a traditional Dutch candle seller. At the back of the shop is **Kramer,** a doll's hospital for both antique and new dolls, and bears, where the doctor (an expert with more than twenty-five years of practice) takes care of these special patients. With its striking window display, **Terra** (*Reestraat 21*) is devoted to Spanish crafts, notably handmade pottery from the different regions as well as classic shoes and boots. If you're approaching De Negen Straatjes from the **Nieuwe Zijde,** you can access the streets via the very picturesque **Heisteeg,** which leads between the houses from the Spui and across the Singel to link up with the Wijde Heisteeg.

de9straatjes.nl • Tram: 2, 12, 13, 17

GOOD **EATS**

■ **CAFÉ AMERICAIN**
Dine in art deco splendor at this hotel restaurant serving modern European dishes, such as risotto with spring vegetables, the classic croque monsieur, and delicious profiteroles.
Amsterdam American Hotel, Leidsekade 97, 1017 PN, 020 556 3010, €€€€

■ **ENVY**
Sleek minimalist design, chic clientele, and top-notch ingredients hit the spot for lunch (try the charcuterie) or dinner (test the tasting menu).
Prinsengracht 381, 1016 HL, 020 344 6407, €€€

■ **T' KUYLTJE**
Well-stuffed Dutch sandwiches (*broodjes*) draw crowds to this modest, busy eatery tucked away off Paleisstraat.
Gasthuismolensteeg 9, 1016 AM, 020 620 1045, €

Woonbootmuseum

10 The *Hendrika Maria* is a converted barge dating from 1913, which then became Amsterdam's Houseboat Museum in 1997. Here you can see how the boat was turned into a cozy home and get a feel for what it's like living on the water. Onboard is a slide show with clips of other houseboats. You can also browse through the books and albums in the living room to find out what's involved in buying, keeping, and maintaining a houseboat.

Prinsengracht 296K, 1016 HW • www.houseboatmuseum.nl • 020 42 70 750 • €
• Closed Mon. (from Jan. to June and from Sep. to Dec), Jan. 1, Jan. 6–22, King's Day, first Sat. of Aug., and Dec. 25, 26 • Tram: 5, 7, 19

Museum van Loon

A stone's throw from the prestigious Gouden Bocht, Keizersgracht 672 epitomizes the grandeur of the Dutch Golden Age.

The Garden Room, with French windows opening out onto a formal garden

The museum takes its name from the van Loon family, owners of the property for more than 100 years. Still operated privately by the family, it is about the grandest canalside house you can visit in Amsterdam. Built in 1672, the double-fronted house was designed by the architect Adriaan Dortsman, and its first resident was one of Rembrandt's more famous students—the painter Ferdinand Bol. The van Loon family acquired the house in 1884, when Hendrik van Loon purchased it for his son Willem as a wedding gift.

Features and Furnishings

The house provides a vivid impression of how the affluent of Amsterdam lived during the 17th and 18th centuries. Whether you're in the **Blue Drawing Room** or the **Red Drawing Room,** going up the grand central staircase, or in one of the bedrooms, you will see that the interior isn't just one style. Instead, it has retained elements from across the years—painted paneling, stucco work, different styles of furniture and wallpaper, and various other period features. There are wonderful fireplaces, mirrors, porcelain vases and plates, silverware, and chandeliers. One of the most attractive rooms is the **Garden Room,** complete with brass dung heater in the fireplace. On some occasions throughout the year, the museum hosts contemporary art exhibitions that blend in with the style of the house.

Family Portraits

As you tour the house, study the van Loon portraits (of which there are more than 80) adorning the walls of the various rooms in the museum.

DON'T **MISS**

When visiting the coach house, don't miss the opportunity to stroll through the beautifully kept garden, with its neatly trimmed geometric hedges and sundial. If your visit coincides with **Open Garden Days** (third weekend in June, www.opengardendays.nl), you'll find other gardens in the area open to the public.

The family originally came from Loon op Zand in North Brabant, and were both wealthy and influential. The family's patriarch, the merchant Willem van Loon, became the founder of the Dutch East India Company (in 1602) and his grandson was the first van Loon to become mayor of Amsterdam.

The Coach House

At one time, many homes in this district also had a coach house. Today, this is the only one where the original unity of canal house, garden, and coach house can be viewed in its entirety. Horses approached it from the parallel Kerkstraat. Its facade was modeled on a Greek temple (note the two niche statues). Inside is a small café, serving drinks and apple pie.

Keizersgracht 672, 1017 ET • www.museumvanloon.nl • 020 624 5255 • € ; guided tours €€€€€ (reservation required) • Closed Jan. 1, King's Day, and Dec. 25 • Metro: Vijzelgracht • Tram: 24

Tulips

Just as iconic as windmills or clogs, tulips play an important role in Dutch economic life today. By far the world's largest exporters of flowers, the Dutch produce an impressive 1.7 billion tulips a year. Whether they are grown for display—as in Keukenhof Park, near the village of Lisse—or as a saleable product, the bright, colorful masses of these splendid flowers are an unmissable springtime spectacle.

Bunches of bright-colored tulips for sale in Amsterdam's Bloemenmarkt
Opposite: National Tulip Day in Dam Square

Exotic Origins

Visitors are often surprised to learn that tulips are not native to the Netherlands. They were introduced to the country more than 400 years ago, in the 1590s, as an exotic curiosity from Turkey. As Europe's most skillful horticulturalists, the Dutch soon made the tulip their own. Growers vied with one another to produce new varieties for the delight of wealthy connoisseurs. Possession of the rarest and most beautiful varieties, such as the *Semper Augustus* and the Viceroy, became a coveted status symbol for the wealthy merchants of Amsterdam and other Dutch cities.

Boom and Bust

We tend to think of the Dutch as prudent, steady, moderate, and level-headed. But about tulips they went completely crazy. In the 1630s, the prices paid for rare bulbs exploded in an infamous outbreak of boom-and-bust speculation. At the height of the tulip mania a *Semper Augustus* bulb was reportedly sold for 10,000 guilders, the value of one of the grandest houses in Amsterdam. One purchaser exchanged almost the entire contents of his farm—oxen, pigs, sheep, wine, butter, cheese, clothes, even a bed—for a single Viceroy bulb. Inevitably, the speculation ended in tears. An irreversible collapse of prices in 1637 left many individuals the ruined owners of a few flowers.

Fields of Color

The key to the fascination of tulips is their intense saturation of hue. In season, which peaks in April or May, depending on the weather, the growing fields within less than an hour's journey of Amsterdam are a blaze of color. You can view the fields by car, on locally rented bicycles, or by bus tour. Or you might decide to visit the renowned tulip beds of **Keukenhof Park** *(Stationsweg 166A, 2161 AM Lisse, www.keukenhof. com, 025 2465 555, €€, open late March to late May).* Established in 1949, Keukenhof claims to be the world's largest flower garden, with seven million bulbs blooming. Also, once a year, the tulips come to Amsterdam. On National Tulip Day in January some 200,000 early tulips are displayed in **Dam Square** as an official start to the season.

Canals

Canals have been a feature of Amsterdam ever since the city was first conceived, and the city has more canals than Venice, as well as no fewer than 1,281 bridges. Whether seen from the water or at street level, the charm of the canals goes hand in hand with the houses that line them and the bridges that span them.

■ Unrivaled Views

The **Seven Bridges** ranged along Reguliersgracht are among Amsterdam's main canal attractions, and are best seen from the water (see p. 145). Be sure to take a boat that goes along Herengracht; you will need good timing to get the perfect photo of the bridges aligned so that they create a tunnel effect as they recede.

The **Grachtengordel** (Canal Ring) does not have a monopoly on the best views. Amsterdam's medieval core has canals that are just as atmospheric. Among them, at the edge of the red-light district, the **Oudezijds Voorburgwal** is the city's oldest canal, dug between 1342 and 1380. It is best viewed from one of its bridges, with the Oude Kerk in the background.

Another classic canal vista takes in the parallel **Geldersekade** from Prins Hendrikkade, with De Waag and the tower of the Zuiderkerk in the distance.

By far the most dramatic view of the Zuiderkerk tower (and arguably one of the best views in all of Amsterdam) is along **Groenburgwal,** seen from the small, white drawbridge that crosses the canal at Staalstraat.

The brick arched bridges constructed at complex junctions are, themselves, attractive features. Check out the narrow radial canals of **Elegantiersgracht** in the Jordaan district or **Reguliersgracht** and **Leidsegracht** of the Southern Canals, which have a more intimate atmosphere.

■ The Best for Wealth

The canals to the west and southwest of the city center reflect the greatest prosperity, lined as they are with some of the city's grandest, 17th-century canalside houses. The broad sweep of Herengracht's **Gouden Bocht** (see p. 137) makes a particularly impressive panorama, best appreciated from one of the bridges that span the canal.

■ Nighttime Treats

The Dutch love to light up their bridges at night. Among the best are the humpbacked bridges along **Prinsengracht** and **Keizersgracht,** whose various arches are lit by hundreds of light bulbs. The **Magere Brug** (see p. 132) that leads from the Amstel River into the Southern Canals district is a particularly lovely sight, whether viewed close-up from the bank or from downstream at the Blauwbrug.

■ Grachtenfestival

Those visiting Amsterdam in August might catch the annual **Canal Festival** *(www.grachtenfestival.nl)*, a 10-day program featuring musical acts, including jazz, opera, and theater, performed on pontoons and in canalside houses, among other venues.

CANAL **CRUISES**

The hop-on, hop-off **Stromma** canal cruise (see p. 176) sells tickets for a day, 24 hours, or 48 hours. They have one line (called the Red line) and you can hop on or off at any of the 8 stops. The company also offers many other options to explore the city by boat. There are also companies with wharves at various strategic points, including the **Lovers** at Centraal Station *(020 530 1090)*, **Rederij Plas** at the Damrak Basin *(020 624 5406)*, and **Rederij Kooij** at the Rokin *(020 623 3810)*.

An impressive 1,200 bulbs illuminate Amsterdam's Magere Brug at night.

MUSEUM DISTRICT
& DE PIJP

Museum District
& de Pijp

Established at the turn of the 20th century, Museumplein (Museum Square) is the epicenter of this district. Three world-class museums flank its grassy terrain—the Rijksmuseum, the Van Gogh Museum, and the Stedelijk Museum. Among them they have literally thousands of Dutch exhibits and works of art on display in their galleries, as well as numerous pieces from farther afield. The museums are all within spitting distance of each other. Also nearby is the classical music venue, the Concertgebouw. Between Museumplein and leafy Vondelpark to the west lies a shopping haven for the elite—P. C. Hooftstraat. In stark contrast, in the Pijp district to the east, the cries of market traders set the tone as people jostle for bargains in one of the city's best-loved and most vibrant street markets.

MUSEUM DISTRICT & DE PIJP

148   **Neighborhood Walk**

158   **In Depth: Rijksmuseum**

162   **In Depth: Van Gogh Museum**

166   **Distinctly Amsterdam: Design Emporiums**

168   **Best Of: Rainy-Day Activities**

❍ **Delft earthenware on display at the Rijksmuseum. Pieces in the collection range from the mid-17th to the 19th century.**

NEIGHBORHOOD **WALK**

① **Rijksmuseum** (see pp. 158–161) **Explore the lavishly renovated national art gallery, then walk behind it and onto grassy Museumplein.**

② **Museumplein** (see p. 150) **Stop for refreshments in this vast square with its splendid vistas, before heading to the entrance of the Stedelijk Museum.**

③ **Stedelijk Museum** (see pp. 150–151) **The intriguing building with a "bathtub" attached has a varied modern and contemporary art collection, as well as an excellent section on design. Cross busy Van Baerlestraat to the Concertgebouw.**

④ **Concertgebouw** (see pp. 83, 151–153) **This impressive building is where the world's best conductors and orchestras play. Pop into the foyer to see what's on during your visit, then head back across Museumplein to the Van Gogh Museum.**

⑤ **Van Gogh Museum** (see pp. 162–165) **Immerse yourself in the world's largest collection of works by the brilliant Dutch painter, then walk along Hobbemastraat until you reach P. C. Hooftstraat.**

MUSEUM DISTRICT & DE PIJP

Map labels:

0 — 400 meters
0 — 400 yards

OVERTOOM
S106
VONDEL STRAAT
STADHOUDERSKADE
CORNELISZOON HOOFTSTRAAT
PIETER
Rijksmuseum ①
PAULUS POTTER STR.
P. C. Hooftstraat ⑥
Van Gogh Museum ⑤
Vondelpark ⑦
Stedelijk Museum ③
Museumplein ②
V. EEGHENSTRAAT
WILLEMSPARKWEG
VAN BREESTRAAT
JACOB
Concertgebouw ④
VAN BAERLESTRAAT
JOHANNES VERHULSTRAAT
OBRECHTSTRAAT
NICOLAAS MAES STR.
FRANS VAN MIERIS STR.
DE LAIRESSESTRAAT
RUYSDAEL STRAAT
ZUID
ROELOF HARLSTRAAT
J. M. COENENSTR.
G. TERBORGSTR.
Noorder
Amstelkanaal

← *CoBrA Museum voor Moderne Kunst, Amsterdamse Bos and Electrische Museumtramlijne*

MUSEUM DISTRICT & DE PIJP DISTANCE: APPROX. 4 MILES (7 KM)
TIME: APPROX. 8 HOURS START: RIJKSMUSEUM

Museum District & de Pijp

The city's world-famous art museums and concert hall converge here.
Find out why this is the cultural heart of Amsterdam.

6 P. C. Hooftstraat (see pp. 153–154) Stroll up the city's most exclusive brand-packed shopping street, then head into Vondelpark.

7 Vondelpark (see pp. 154–155) After visiting the hidden treasures of this 19th-century park, exit by the bridge at Van Baerlestraat, walk past the Concertgebouw, and turn left at Ruysdaelstraat, which leads into Albert Cuypstraat.

MUSEUM DISTRICT & DE PIJP

8 Albert Cuypmarkt (see pp. 105, 156) This street market evokes all the senses. Soak up the atmosphere, then retrace your steps—or cut through—to Ferdinand Bolstraat and walk north until a huge brick brewery comes into sight.

9 Heineken Experience (see pp. 156–157) Discover all there is to know about making this premium brand and complete your tour with a chilled glass of beer.

Map labels:
Boerenwetering
H. M. V. RANDWIJK-PLANTSOEN
Heineken Experience
Singelgracht
SARPHATI STRAAT
OOSTEINDE
WESTEINDE
STADHOUDERSKADE
TORONTO-BRUG
FRANS HALS STRAAT
MARIE HEINEKEN-PLEIN
ALBERT CUYPSTRAAT
VAN JAN STEEN STR.
TWEEDE
WOUSTRACHT
AMSTELDIJK
NIEUWE AMSTEL-BRUG
RUYSDAELKADE
Albert Cuypmarkt
DE PIJP
SARPHATI-PARK
CEINTUURBAAN
Amstel
EERSTE JAN STEEN STR.
SARPHATI- PARK
VAN
OSTADESTRAAT
RUSTENBURGER- STRAAT
TOLSTRAAT
TOLSTRAAT
CEINTUURBAAN
RUYSDAELKADE
HENRICK DE KEIJSER-PLEIN
VAN WOUSTRACHT
SMARAGD-PLEIN
TALMASTR.
DE DAGERAAD
H. R.-PLEIN
ISRAELSKADE
T. S.-PLEIN
PIETER LODEWIJK TAAKSTR.
JOZEF
AMSTELKADE
Amstelkanaal

MUSEUM DISTRICT & DE PIJP

Rijksmuseum

1 See pp. 158–161.

Museumstraat 1, 1071 XX • www.rijksmuseum.nl • 020 6747 000 • €€
• Tram: 1, 2, 5, 7, 12, 19

Museumplein

2 The cultural heart of Amsterdam, Museum Square is the big back garden of the **Rijksmuseum** (see pp. 158–161), the **Van Gogh Museum** (see pp. 162–165), and the **Stedelijk Museum** (see below). It was officially laid in 1903 to a revised 1891 plan by P. J. H. Cuypers, the architect of the Rijksmuseum. Pause here to take photos of the stunning views between museum visits, or head to the **Cobra Café** *(Hobbemastraat 18, www.cobracafe.nl, 020 470 0111)*. In perfect symmetry with the **Museum Shop,** the café is the work of Swedish architect Sven-Ingvar Andersson, who redesigned the square in 1999. His legacy also includes an underground supermarket with a sloping grass roof, which provides an imaginative spot for picnicking (see p. 16). Crowds swarm into the square on national holidays, including King's Day and Liberation Day, for cultural events, and during major football competitions, when a big screen is set up outdoors. There's also a basketball court, a skate park, and a shallow pool that becomes an ice-skating rink in winter—if the temperature drops below freezing.

Looking across Museumplein. This open space—Museum Square—hosted the International Colonial and Export Exhibition in 1883. Today it is home to three major museums—the Rijksmuseum (seen in the distance above), the Van Gogh Museum, and the Stedelijk Museum.

Van Baerlestraat •Tram: 1, 2, 5, 7, 12, 19

Stedelijk Museum

3 Founded in 1874, Amsterdam's museum of modern and contemporary art and design was originally housed in the Rijksmuseum.

However, in 1895, it moved into its own neo-Renaissance building, designed by Dutch architect Adriaan Willem Weissman. The Stedelijk Museum closed for an extensive renovation in the first decade of the 21st century, lasting nine years. It reopened in 2012, with

A wall drawing by the American artist Sol LeWitt at the Stedelijk Museum of modern and contemporary art and design

the addition of a brand-new wing—nicknamed **The Bathtub** for reasons that will become obvious when you see it.

Bright, airy, and spacious inside, the museum is a pleasure to walk around, and an absolute must if you are a fan of modern art and design. A world-class permanent collection combines with quirky installations and inspired temporary exhibitions. You'll find all the major art and design movements since the early 20th century represented here, and with an impressive roll call of featured artists: Marc Chagall, Wassily Kandinsky, Henri Matisse, Jackson Pollock, Karel Appel, Andy Warhol, and Willem de Kooning among many others. Highlights include a stunning design section focusing on work by the Dutch modernist architect H. P. Berlage and celebrated American designers Charles and Ray Eames. Every artwork is described adequately in English, but get an audio tour by all means. And if time is short, restrict your visit to homegrown talent, viewing the collections on the De Stijl and CoBrA art movements.

Museumplein 10, 1071 DJ • www.stedelijk.nl • 020 573 2911 • €€ • Tram: 2, 3, 5, 12

Concertgebouw

4 A tour de force of Viennese classicism, this palatial classical music venue was designed by Dutch architect Adolf van Gendt who, together with P. J. H. Cuypers, drew up the plans for **Centraal Station** (see p. 48). The elevated glass-centric foyer that

MUSEUM DISTRICT & DE PIJP

juts out at the side of the main building was designed by Pi de Bruijn and added toward the end of the 1980s, in order to cope with the increasing number of visitors. It's hard to imagine now, but when the first stone was laid in 1883, the site was no more than a muddy field that lay just beyond the city's boundaries. Now it's one of the world's busiest concert halls, staging a staggering 800 or so concerts annually, attracting the crème de la crème of international musicians and conductors, and a voracious public. Audrey Hepburn even had a season ticket when she lived in Amsterdam following World War II.

According to his family, van Gendt lacked any musical ability, yet he was somehow able to create a perfectly resonant hall in the main auditorium, the **Grote Zaal.** Those of the smaller, oval-shaped **Kleine Zaal** are perfectly suited for chamber concerts. Time your visit to coincide with a free 30-minute lunchtime concert *(Wed. 12:30 p.m., except July and Aug.),* affording an

The Grote Zaal ("big hall") at the Concertgebouw is recognized for its outstanding acoustics.

exclusive glimpse of some of the world's finest conductors and orchestras at work, including the venue's world-renowned resident classical music orchestra and resident jazz orchestra. Alternatively, join a 75-minute guided tour of the building, given in English (€€€; Sun. 12:30 p.m., Wed. 1:30 p.m., Fri. 5 p.m.; from May to Sep., Mon. 5 p.m.). If you plan to attend a concert here on another night of your visit, pop into the foyer and check out the venue's program of evening events.

Concertgebouwplein 10, 1071 LN • www.concertgebouw.nl • 020 671 8345 • €€€€€; guided tours €€ • Tram: 2, 3, 5, 12, 16, 24

SAVVY **TRAVELER**

With three substantial museums to visit, this tour is compact. As an alternative to having lunch somewhere, take short breaks en route for energy-boosting snacks. All the sites between the museums—Museumplein, P. C. Hooftstraat, Vondelpark, and Albert Cuypmarkt—offer numerous opportunities for coffee breaks, light bites, and mid-afternoon treats. You can always indulge at dinner later on.

Van Gogh Museum

5 See pp. 162–165.

Museumplein 6, 1071 CX • www.vangoghmuseum.nl • 020 570 5200 • €€ • Tram: 2, 3, 5, 12

P. C. Hooftstraat

6 The city's most exclusive shopping street emerged in 1876 as the city continued to expand concentrically. It was named after the aristocratic 16th-century Dutch poet, playwright, and historian Pieter Corneliszoon Hooft (considered one of the founders of the literary culture in the Netherlands), and for a century was filled with local bookstores, butchers, and grocers serving the district's upper-class residents. However, increasingly high rents forced the traders out of business and, at the beginning of the 1980s, luxury stores began moving into the 1,150-foot (350 m) stretch between Hobbemastraat and Van Baerlestraat. As you start to walk up the street—past a couple of rather incongruous

GOOD **EATS**

■ **CONSERVATORIUM**
It would be difficult to find a nicer place to have lunch. Enjoy your fare in the internal courtyard surrounded by spectacular floor-to-ceiling windows.
Van Baerlestraat 27, 1071 AN, 020 570 0000, €€€

■ **SAMA SEBO**
Restaurant Sama Sebo is the oldest Indonesian specialty restaurant in the Netherlands.
P. C. Hooftstraat, 1071 BL, 020 662 8146, €€–€€€

■ **THE SEAFOOD BAR**
Appetizing, fresh seafood dishes, including fish and chips and fruits de mer, served in a clean and bright interior.
Van Baerlestraat 5, 1071 AL, 020 670 8355, €€–€€€

souvenir stores—you'll see the storefronts of familiar international brands, like **Emporio Armani** (*Nos. 39–41*), **Mulberry** (*No. 46*), **Gucci** (*Nos. 56–58*), **Jimmy Choo** (*No. 62*), and various other usual suspects. But before turning the corner into this stretch, dive into **G-Star** (*No. 28*), a Dutch designer brand that makes vintage, military-inspired, urban clothing. And to see signature collections by Paloma Picasso, the youngest daughter of the famous Spanish painter, pop into **Tiffany & Co.** (*Nos. 86–88*). Check out **Oger** (*No. 75–81*) if you are looking for shirts and suits. Walk by **Louis Vuitton** (*No. 65–67*) and **Chanel** (*No. 66*), before finding respite—both for you and your credit cards—by walking to the end of the street and into Vondelpark.

www.pchooftstraat.nl • Tram: 2, 3, 5, 12

Vondelpark

7 Vondelpark is to Amsterdam what Central Park is to New York. However, despite increasingly strict regulations about where you're allowed to barbecue or walk your dog, it still attracts millions of visitors annually, among them sun-seekers, picnickers, joggers, footballers, in-line skaters, and dog-walkers. It's also used by cyclists to whiz from the center of town to the south. When this 120-acre (48.5 ha) haven of green opened in 1865, it was simply known as Nieuwe Park (New Park), before being renamed after the city's famous writer and playwright Joost van den Vondel. As you enter the park, you should see a pond in front of you. Follow the path to the other side of it, to the modernist **Blauwe Theehuis** (*www.blauwetheehuis.nl, 020 235 7170, €*). Resembling a flying saucer, the park's 1937 architectural icon was the work of brothers

Designed in 1865, Vondelpark attracts 10 million visitors each year.

H. A. J. and Jan Baanders. When the sun's out, the cool and cool-at-heart come in their droves to hang out on its peaceful terraces until late into the evening. Next door is an **open-air theater** *(www. openluchttheater.nl)* that comes to life in the summer months with Dutch cabaret, comedy, music, and dance: It's free, so you can pop in and out at whim. If you have children, walk on to the **Groot Melkhuis** *(www.grootmelkhuis.nl, 020 612 9674, €)*, a family-friendly café with an adjoining playground. At the southern end of the park is **Vondeltuin** *(www.vondeltuin.nl, 06 2756 5576, €€)*, a laid-back outdoor bar and restaurant with plenty of lounging potential on its chunky wooden furniture. Walk back to the northern corner of the park and you'll pass the Italian Renaissance-style **Vondelpark Pavilion,** built by architect W. Hamer between 1874 and 1881, the recently acquired home of Dutch public broadcasting association, AVRO.

Tram: 1, 2, 3, 12

Albert Cuypmarkt

8 The origin of this market goes all the way back to fin de siècle Amsterdam. Between 1898 and 1900, de Zaagmolensloot (Sawmill Ditch) was filled in to create the street now known as Albert Cuypstraat—named after the 17th-century painter Albert Cuyp. The picturesque waterway, lined with the windmills of timber merchants, had fallen prey to the expansion of the city. Soon, market traders and hawkers with handcarts descended on the street, purveying their wares illegally to the newly ensconced population. It wasn't until 1905 that the city allowed the market to operate officially—but only on Saturday evenings. In 1912, trade extended to every day apart from Sunday. The market thrived, surviving the economic crisis of the 1930s, but suffered badly when around one-third of its traders—the Jewish—were deported during World War II. As virtually none returned, a somber mood hung over the market for years. Then, the vibrant 1960s and 1970s breathed new life into the market and it slowly reinvented itself as the cheap and cheerful, colorful, and multicultural trading area that it is to this day. Wander up the long street sampling cheese and freshly made *stroopwafels* (see pp. 126–127), giggling at some of the more tacky fashion items along the way, and, if you like sewing, admiring the impressive selection of fabrics.

Albert Cuypstraat • www.albertcuypmarkt.nl • Closed Sun., June 4, 5 and Dec. 25, 26 • Tram: 3, 4, 24

The city's largest street market, Albert Cuypmarkt, runs for more than half a mile (1 km) in Amsterdam's de Pijp district. You'll find everything here from fresh fruits and vegetables, to artisan breads and cheeses, to textiles and homewares.

Heineken Experience

9 In 1864, Gerard Adriaan Heineken bought the Hooiberg brewery on the Nieuwezijds Voorburgwal and the story of one of the world's most famous beer brands began. Three years later, Heineken built a large, brick brewery on the Stadhouderskade, which is where the Heineken

Among the highlights of the Heineken Experience is this vast, tiled brewing room.

Experience—spread over four floors—is housed *(last admission: 5:30 p.m. Mon.–Thurs.; 6:30 p.m. Fri.–Sat.)*. An immersive, interactive journey through the history of the brand and the brewing process, the exhibition is engaging, informative—and yes, a little cheesy in places. You'll learn how Heineken's special proprietary yeast was developed by a student of Louis Pasteur, see the original copper kettles used for brewing the beer, and visit the immaculately groomed shire horses who pull carts piled with barrels of beer around town, purely for show. You can also create your own video—to the soundtrack of "Tulips in Amsterdam," if you like—and undergo the entire brewing process as an ingredient in the imaginative **Brew You simulation ride.** The tour ends with two complimentary beers in the **World Bar,** where a virtual beer mat appears whenever you put your glass down. Not a bad way to end the day.

Stadhouderskade 78, 1072 AE • www.heinekenexperience.com • 020 261 1323 • €€
• Metro: Vijzelgracht • Tram: 1, 7, 19, 24

Rijksmuseum

A ten-year restoration, completed in 2013, breathed new life and light into the most famous museum in the Netherlands.

Adriaen de Vries's striking bronze of the sea god Triton (ca 1615–1618)

Originally the work of 19th-century architect Pierre Cuypers, the galleries housing this world-famous collection of Dutch art and artifacts now benefit from a modern reworking of light and space. The collection, too, has been expanded, restored, and rethought. Displayed in 80 galleries over four floors, it presents a lucid, chronological overview of Dutch art and its influence, from Jan van Scorel's richly clad "Mary Magdalene" (1530) and Rembrandt's "The Night Watch" to an actual FK 23 Bantam aircraft.

Atrium

This new, two-part entrance hall in the basement, Level 0, presents visitors with their first breathtaking sight—the work of Spanish architects Cruz y Ortiz, who here redesigned, and elsewhere restored, the original building. They moved galleries to open up inner courtyards, lowered floors, and hung immense chandelier-like structures overhead to diffuse the natural light from the glass roof. No ticket is needed to admire this space, though you will find ticket sales here, the cloakroom, a café, and a shop.

Renaissance Art

Galleries at Level 0 present paintings from the Middle Ages and Renaissance in Italy and the Netherlands. The eponymous work by the Master of the Virgo inter Virgines is a remarkable expression of female tenderness, while Piero Torrigiani's terra-cotta bust of **"The Virgin as Mater Dolorosa"** (ca 1500–1510) offers another touching view of maternal devotion. Sumptuous and considerably less sorrowful is the sophisticated depiction of **"Mary Magdalene"** by Jan van Scorel, considered the first Netherlandish artist to make the aims of Italian Renaissance art his own.

SAVVY **TRAVELER**

Once you have seen Level 0, the easiest way to orient yourself around the remaining galleries is from Level 2, the heart of the museum. It connects the four corners of the building and gives the best access to the different parts of the collection, including the only access to the 20th-century galleries on Level 3.

Gallery of Honor

From Level 0, head straight to Level 2 (see Savvy Traveler, above). Here, more than 30 galleries celebrate the Golden Age of Dutch art in the 17th century, when this tiny maritime republic became a world power. The long **Gallery of Honor** forms the backbone of the entire collection. Beautifully showcased against gray walls in side alcoves and softly lit from above, portraits, still lifes, and genre paintings by the Flemish and Dutch masters come to life. They include two prized acquisitions, Jan Steen's **"A Burgomaster of Delft and his Daughter"** (1655) and the arresting landscape **"The 'Golden Bend' in the Herengracht"** (1671–1672) by Gerrit Berckheyde, along with Frans Hals's **"Merry Drinker"** (ca 1628). Also here, are several works of one of the world's least prolific of all artists, Johannes

Vermeer. In his lifetime, he produced only about 35 paintings whose unique quality was not recognized until the 19th century. Two such jewels are "**The Milkmaid**" (ca 1658), mesmerizing for its small size, textural quality, and lustrous coloring, and "**Woman Reading a Letter** "(1663). Alongside these hangs the much-loved "**Little Street**" (ca 1658), one of only two outdoor scenes by this enigmatic artist.

The goal at the end of the Gallery of Honor is Rembrandt's "**The Night Watch**" (1642), the huge, and hugely famous, group portrait of local militia once called "a thunderbolt of genius." It is currently undergoing one of the most important restoration projects

DON'T **MISS**

While on Level 2, take a peek in gallery 2.20, which displays 17th-century dollhouses once owned by two of Amsterdam's wealthy women collectors, Petronella Oortman and Petronella Dunois. Made to scale, they show exactly what the town houses of the wealthy were like. In fact, Oortman went to such lengths to furnish her dollhouse with exquisite miniature items of glass, silverware, furniture, and pictures, that it eventually cost her as much money as an actual canal-side house would have done.

of all times. Visitors can see the painting, which is protected by a large, glass display chamber, and follow the restoration in real time as scholars and restorers do their work. The project is called Operation Nightwatch (you can follow its progress at the museum website). Other Rembrandt riches include "**The Jewish Bride**" (ca 1665) and the shadowy, mop-headed "**Self-portrait at an Early Age**" (ca 1628).

■ 20th Century

On Level 3, at the top of the museum, new galleries hold some interesting, if eclectic, recent acquisitions, such as the oldest Dutch-designed airplane, the "**Bantam**" (1917); the rare white **Armchair** designed for Til Brugman (1923) by Gerrit Rietveld; and Karel Appel's CoBrA art movement painting, "**The Square Man**" (1951).

Rotating photographic displays here draw on the museum's enormous collection of 19th- and 20th-century photographs, which includes work by the celebrated Hungarian, László Moholy-Nagy, among others.

■ Cuypers Library

Before leaving the museum to explore its beautiful gardens, make your way to Level 1, to the magnificent art library by Pierre Cuypers. The library

Rembrandt's "The Night Watch," renowned for its complex use of light and shadow

has been restored to its original state and remains a splendid example of the architect's richly decorative, yet graceful, interior design. The library's reading room is open to the public and visitors will find iPads for browsing the museum collection further, as well as free Wi-Fi access.

■ Outdoor Museum

The gardens surrounding the museum, also revamped with the original Cuypers design in mind, offer a welcome rest and yet more aesthetic pleasures, with exhibits of international sculpture and a brand new Asian Pavilion. Surrounded by water, this houses the museum's collection of Asian art dating back to 2000 B.C. and includes a pair of imposing 14th-century Japanese wooden temple guardians.

Museumstraat 1, 1071 XX • www.rijksmuseum.nl • 020 6747 000 • €€ • Tram: 1, 2, 5, 7, 12, 19

MUSEUM DISTRICT & DE PIJP

Van Gogh Museum

More than 200 paintings and 400 drawings by the celebrated artist are assembled in this popular museum.

Among the paintings in the permanent collection are "The Harvest" and "Sunflowers."

A light-filled, splendidly refurbished building designed by the modernist architect Gerrit Rietveld houses the world's largest collection of works by Vincent van Gogh. A wide selection of these hang chronologically on the first floor, telling the story of van Gogh's life and artistic development with an emphasis on the last four years of intense activity that produced his most famous paintings. Also on view are works by the Impressionists and Post-impressionists, while the adjoining Exhibition Wing presents temporary shows.

Early Years

For van Gogh art was a spiritual vocation, which he discovered in 1880, at the age of 27. It was a means, he believed, of bringing consolation to the world. He initially concentrated on drawing and took peasants as his subjects, experimenting with all kinds of media, such as black chalk and pen and ink. His early oil paintings similarly used a very dark palette and led in 1885 to **"The Potato Eaters,"** in which the faces have, according to van Gogh, "the color of a good, dusty potato, unpeeled naturally."

Paris 1886–1888

A move to Paris, city of the Impressionists, triggered a major change in the artist's work. He started using a much lighter palette and a broken, Impressionistic style of brushwork, which can be seen in **"Boulevard de Clichy"** (1887), showing the street in Montmartre where he stayed. Van Gogh met and befriended other artists and shared the contemporary enthusiasm for Japanese prints. He also embarked on one of his abiding themes: self-portraiture. Of the 29 such pieces from this period, **"Self-portrait as a Painter"** (1888) is a rarity in showing van Gogh at his easel.

A Year in Arles 1888–1889

Seeking better light and color, van Gogh arrived in Provence in February 1888, to be greeted by freezing weather. Though confined indoors, he plunged into painting and from now on poured out hundreds of works, including those for which he is best known. Many portray his immediate surroundings, such as **"The Yellow House,"** where he lived, and **"The Bedroom."** Others show the impact of spring and the influence of Japanese printmaking, as in **"Small Pear Tree in Blossom"** and **"The Pink Orchard."** With the arrival of summer he was able to work outdoors, which inspired the vividly yellow landscape, **"The Harvest."**

"Sunflowers" 1888

Van Gogh both saw and used color as an emotional force, and for him yellow signified love. It features most

MUSEUM DISTRICT & DE PIJP

DON'T **MISS**

Keep an eye out for examples of the artist's letters. Van Gogh wrote prolifically to friends, fellow artists, and especially to his brother, Theo, who sent him money and materials in exchange for paintings. The letters give a rich insight into his working practice and his personality–and reveal him to be a highly cultured man who loved words almost as much as he loved color.

famously in his **"Sunflowers"** series, which he painted in August 1888—all "in one rush," because the flowers faded so quickly. Anticipating the arrival of Paul Gauguin to share his studio, he wanted these pictures to hang in his friend's room. Gauguin's visit ended disastrously, however, with an overwrought van Gogh suffering a breakdown. Just weeks later, though, van Gogh made three "quietly composed repetitions" of these still lifes, of which one is on view here.

■ St-Rémy 1889–1890

In May 1889, after two more acute mental crises, van Gogh admitted himself to a psychiatric hospital in the village of St-Rémy, near Arles. He spent a year there and produced 150 paintings—many of them

now considered masterpieces—in addition to a number of drawings. Despite his precarious mental state, his eye and hand remained assured. This can clearly be seen in **"Olive Grove,"** one of ten paintings of the silvery trees that fascinated the artist; **"The Garden of St. Paul's Hospital;"** and **"Irises,"** a glorious concoction of purple against lemon yellow. The luminous **"Almond Blossom"** was a gift to his brother, Theo, on the birth of his child.

■ Last Months 1890

Settling in Auvers-sur-Oise, north of Paris, to be near Theo, van Gogh continued to paint at a furious pace, concentrating on the surrounding landscape. **"Wheatfield with Crows,"** with its disturbed lines and menacing bird shapes, dates from the very last month of his life, July 1890. It may or may not be his last work, but shortly afterward van Gogh shot himself fatally and died.

■ Impressionist Works

Works by the great Impressionists are displayed on the third floor. The freedom of color and brushwork that dominates these paintings had a lasting influence on van Gogh. He probably knew Claude Monet's

The vivid yellows of van Gogh's "Sunset" feature frequently in many of his works.

"Bulb Fields near The Hague" (1886), since this and several other pictures by Monet were handled by his art dealer brother, Theo. Van Gogh also found fellow Parisian Camille Pissarro very inspiring and much admired his experiment in pointillism, **"The Haymaking, Éragny"** (1887).

◾ Paul Gauguin
Despite their differences, Paul Gauguin ranks with van Gogh as one of the world's greatest Postimpressionist painters. Appropriately, his pictures here include **"Van Gogh Painting Sunflowers"** (1888), a work of pure imagination, along with the very fine **"Self-Portrait with Portrait of Bernard"** (1888), which he sent to van Gogh in advance of his visit to Arles. **"Breton Girl Spinning"** (1889) is a delightful example of his work in Brittany, where he belonged to the artists' colony at Pont-Aven.

Museumplein 6, 1071 CX • www.vangoghmuseum.nl • 020 570 5200 • €€ • Tram: 2, 3, 5, 12

Design Emporiums

For a small nation, the Dutch have a big reputation when it comes to design. They are renowned for their simplicity and minimalism which, combined with out-of-the-box thinking, create a potent tour de force. But it's the dry sense of humor that imbues each design that makes it distinctly Dutch. And here, in a city renowned for creativity and commerce, there's plenty on offer.

Groundbreaking Stores

First stop on any design tour should be **Droog** (*Staalstraat 7B, www.droog.com, 020 523 5050*), meaning "dry." This design company creates cutting-edge products, projects, and events all over the world and is rightfully credited with pioneering new directions for design. It produced Marcel Wanders's iconic Knotted Chair in 1996—since an acquisition in the permanent collection of New York's MoMA—and its ground-floor exhibition space within a 17th-century building, once home to the textile guild, captures the design zeitgeist perfectly. Upstairs, design aficionados can spend the night in **Hôtel Droog**, a one-bedroom attic apartment, or enjoy breakfast, lunch, high tea, or dinner in the bright and spacious **Cafe@droog**. The design store that started it

Minimalist housewares for sale at Droog's flagship store. Opposite: The Mobilia Woonstudio, selling contemporary home furnishings in the Southern Canals district

all, however, is **Frozen Fountain** (*Prinsengracht 645, www.frozenfountain.nl, 020 622 9375*), founded in 1985 by Dick Dankers. Here you'll find one-off items and limited editions by prominent contemporary designers such as Jurgen Bey, Hella Jongerius, and Piet Hein Eek—the latter known for working with reclaimed wood long before recycling was trendy. The store also showcases the work of up-and-coming artists. **Moooi** (*Westerstraat 187, www.moooi. com, 020 528 7760*)—which means "beautiful" in Dutch, with an extra "o" thrown in—is an internationally renowned design label cofounded by Marcel Wanders in 2001. Its showroom features playful, daring, and larger-than-life creations from national and international designers.

Must-have Accessories

De Negen Straatjes (see pp. 138–139) is a treasure trove of Dutch design, but you have to hunt it out. World-famous Amsterdam designer **Hester van Eeghen** has two shops selling her brightly colored, geometric designs—one for shoes (*Hartenstraat 1, 020 626 9211*) and one for bags (*Hartenstraat 37, 020 626 9213*).

(see pp. 138–139)

DIME-STORE **DESIGN**

Something of an institution in the Netherlands, **HEMA** (*www.hema.nl, 020 422 8988*) was opened as an experimental dime store during the economic crisis of the 1920s. Today, the now-international retail chain carries good quality, affordable products that are the epitome of Dutch design: practical, simple, and brightly colored. The chain has several stores dotted around town.

MUSEUM DISTRICT & DE PIJP

Rainy-Day Activities

It has to be said: Amsterdam isn't exactly known for its great weather. Instead, it has a typical western European climate, which means a fair bit of rainfall throughout the year. However, there is still plenty to do in this cultural city to make sure that rain doesn't have to stop play.

■ American Hotel

If plans for a picnic in **Vondelpark** (see pp. 154–155) are rained out, head instead to American Hotel just a few streets away. You don't have to be a resident to eat in the historic **Café Americain** here. Built in 1902, Amsterdam architect Willem Kromhout's stunning art nouveau interior retains its Parisian chic atmosphere. Opt for classic brasserie dishes—a club sandwich, croque monsieur, beef croquettes—while you wait for those clouds to pass.

Leidsekade 97, 1017 PN • www.cafeamericain.nl • 020 556 3010 • €€€€ • Tram: 1, 2, 5, 7, 12, 19

■ Zuiderbad

If you don't care much for the rain but do like water, this is the place to get soaked. Situated in the Pijp district and housed in a building dating from 1897, this art nouveau swimming pool—complete with a fountain—is undoubtedly the city's most stylish public pool. Founded in 1911, it was renovated in 2013 and now boasts whirlpools, herbal baths, and a wellness corner.

Hobbemastraat 26, 1071 ZC • www.zuid. amsterdam.nl • 020 252 1390 • €€ • Tram: 2, 5, 12

■ Hermitage Amsterdam

Around 300 years ago, Tsar Peter the Great visited Amsterdam and drew inspiration from the city when founding St. Petersburg. It is fitting, then, that Amsterdam has this satellite museum of the world-famous Hermitage in Russia (see pp. 132–134). Situated in the Southern Canals district, the museum holds inspired temporary exhibitions, usually featuring a wealth of Russian treasures. It also has three permanent exhibitions in the Amstel wing. There's also a smart

Temporary exhibitions at Hermitage Amsterdam regularly present collections that epitomize the wealth of the former Russian Empire.

café-restaurant on the first floor, right over the foyer, in which to sip champagne or drink a cup of coffee; it's a real rain-beater.

Amstel 51, 1018 EJ • www.hermitage.nl • 020 530 8758 • €€€ • Closed King's Day and Dec. 25 • Metro: Waterlooplein • Tram: 14

■ Pathé Tuschinski

Chase the rainy-day blues away by watching the latest Hollywood blockbusters in the main auditorium of one of the world's most beautiful cinemas, located in the Southern Canals district. The Tuschinski was originally built in 1921 by cinephile Abraham Icek Tuschinski, a Jewish tailor from Poland who perished in Auschwitz during World War II. The building's extraordinary twin-towered facade and sumptuous carpeted interior present an eclectic jumble of art deco, art nouveau, and Amsterdam School styles. The likes of Charlie Chaplin and Harold Lloyd presented their films here. You can take a tour to see the beautiful screening rooms and discover tidbits about the most notable guests that have visited the cinema (every day, 9:30 – 11:30 a.m., € 10, price includes coffee or tea).

Reguliersbreestraat 26–28, 1017 CN • en.pathe.nl • €€€ • Tram: 4, 16, 24

■ Sauna Deco

Soak up a 1920s Parisian atmosphere at this decorative sauna in the Northern Canals district. Many of its art deco features—including stained-glass windows and intricately patterned railings—were rescued from Paris department store Le Bon Marché. Services include the usual facilities, plus massage and manicure, for a mixed-gender clientele.

Herengracht 115, 1015 BE • www.sauna deco.nl • 020 623 8215 • €€€ • Tram: 2, 12, 13, 17

■ Tropenmuseum

A rainy day will afford you the time to wander through this vast, three-floored museum of anthropology in the Jodenbuurt district. Its rich collection of art and objects—many displayed in reconstructed scenes—together with photographs, music, and film bring to life diverse cultures from all over the world. Then head across the road to the superb beer bar, De Biertuin *(Linneausstraat 29, www.debiertuin.nl, 020 665 0956),* to sample another kind of culture. A perfect destination if you have

Theater Tuschinski is a throwback to the golden age of movie theaters.

children (the "Junior" section of the museum is remarkable).

Linnaeusstraat 2 • www.tropenmuseum.nl • 088 0042 800 • €€ • Closed Jan. 1, King's Day, Dec. 25, Mon. (except July–Aug., Oct. 14 and 21, Dec. 23 and 30) • Tram: 3, 7, 14, 19

■ TunFun

Stuck for something to do with the kids? Thankfully, Amsterdam has the perfect antidote: TunFun. This gigantic children's playground is located in the Jodenbuurt district, within a former tunnel that runs below the Meester Visserplein. Kids have an array of adventurous climbing structures at their disposal, as well as slides, inflatables, and a special toddlers' section. Meanwhile, parents can relax and have something hot (coffee or tea) to drink.

Meester Visserplein 7, 1011 RD • www.tunfun.nl • 020 689 4300 • €, no cash • Closed Mon. and Tue., Jan. 1, King's Day, and Dec. 25 • Metro: Waterlooplein • Tram: 9, 14

■ Amsterdam Public Library

Despite its rather nondescript exterior, the **Openbare Bibliotheek Amsterdam (OBA)** resembles a contemporary art museum inside: white space, high ceilings, colorful designer furniture, and Apple computers. Located in the Oosterdok area, near Centraal Station, it boasts 15 miles (25 km) of books—including plenty in English—an inexhaustible selection of international magazines, and a huge choice of DVDs and CDs. On the ground floor, there's a piano that anyone can play, as long as they're good. You can pretty much move in here on a rainy day. There's a café (OBA Café) on the ground floor, serving coffees and bagels; at the top of the building—with a great view across Amsterdam—is the restaurant **Babel** (*www.babel.amsterdam, 020 523 0870*).

Oosterdokskade 143, 1011 DL • www.oba.nl • 020 523 0900 • Metro: Centraal Station • Tram: 2, 4, 12, 14, 26

■ De Prael

There are worse things you can do when it starts to pour than head to this spacious, yet snug, *proeflokaal* (tasting house) in the Oude Zijde district. Settle in and sample its delicious organic beers produced from hops grown in the garden behind. All are named after famous Dutch crooners, are of varying strengths, and are utterly delicious. Beer enthusiasts can also take a tour of its **brewery** (*Oudezijds Voorburgwal 30, 020 408 4470, €€–€€€€, p.m. tours, closed Sat., Sun.*).

Oudezijds Armsteeg 26, 1012 GP • www.deprael. nl • 020 408 4469 • Metro: Centraal Station or Nieuwmarkt • Tram: 2, 4, 12, 14, 26

PART 3

Travel Essentials

PLANNING YOUR TRIP

When To Go
Amsterdam is what you make of it, but some seasons are particularly good for specific interests—be they traditional events, gardens, festivals, or fine weather.

January and February are ideal months for good-value accommodations, relatively empty restaurants and museums, and winter sales.

Visiting Amsterdam in **March and April** guarantees you a blaze of glorious tulips, daffodils, and crocuses. A visit to Keukenhof Park (see p. 143) and a drive or bike ride through the bulb fields makes for an unforgettable spring. Easter, which may fall in March or April, brings age-old Dutch traditions and spellbinding music to Amsterdam's churches. On April 27, Amsterdam goes orange to celebrate King's Day with carnival atmosphere consuming the entire city.

In **May,** Amsterdam joins the rest of the Netherlands when its citizens pause to pay their respects to the fallen soldiers of World War II and more recent military conflicts and peacekeeping operations on Herdenkingsdag (Remembrance Day, May 4). Then it's time for a national party on May 5, as people take to the streets to celebrate their freedom on Bevrijdingsdag (Liberation Day).

The Holland Festival of performing arts runs through most of **June** and Open Tuinen Dagen (Open Garden Days) takes place on the third weekend of June, enabling you to gain access to private homes and gardens. Come **July** in Amsterdam, summer is in full swing: The city beaches host dance music events, the Robeco Summer Concert Series returns to the Concertgebouw, and festival season starts in earnest. **August** kicks off with Gay Pride before heading into the classical music Grachtenfestival (Canal Festival) and multi-event Uitmarkt.

Clinging to the last rays of sunshine in **September,** Amsterdam still offers plenty in the way of festivals, such as the Dutch Theater Festival and accompanying Fringe Festival, and the Valtifest music event in Noord. This can be a delightful month to visit, with fewer tourists and crisp autumnal days. As nights draw in come **October,** events head indoors, such as the Cinekid Festival and Amsterdam Dance Event, the world's biggest club festival.

The winter months, **November and December,** are when Dutch *gezelligheid* (conviviality) comes into its own. The long, cold days are made bearable by hunkering down in cozy, candlelit cafés and beautifully decorated shops and hotels. With the hotly anticipated Sinterklaas Intocht (Feast of St. Nicholas) on December 5, Christmas and New Year's Eve just around

the corner, this is the time to embrace Amsterdam's winter traditions: chocolate letters, *pepernoten* (gingerbread cookies) and *speculaas* cookies, mulled wine, Christmas markets, ice-skating, and holiday concerts and plays.

Climate
In Amsterdam they say that the weather has only three states: If it's not already raining, then it has either just stopped or is just about to start. In truth, it doesn't rain quite so much but the city's maritime climate does result in fairly frequent overcast days. Those cloudy Dutch skies were a great inspiration to landscape painters of the Dutch Golden Age, but to modern travelers, they are a warning not to travel far without a light, waterproof coat or an umbrella.

Somber weather generally prevails in **spring,** yet spirits soar perceptibly during **summer,** when temperatures can rise above 80°F (25°C) and Amsterdammers become Mediterranean, making the most of the fair weather by eating and drinking outdoors as much as possible. **Fall** can also be delightful, with blue skies and fluffy clouds and a riot of autumnal foliage along the canals. **Winter** can bring freezing sea fog that hangs over the city for a day at a time. As soon as the wind changes to an easterly direction, the fog blows away and is replaced by cold, blue skies. Snow and deep frost are now rare, because the city has such a warm microclimate.

Insurance
Take out enough travel insurance to cover emergency medical treatment, loss or theft, and repatriation.

Passports
U.S. and Canadian citizens may stay in the Netherlands for up to three months with just a valid passport. No visas are required.

HOW TO GET TO AMSTERDAM

By Airplane
Amsterdam's **Schiphol airport** (*www.schiphol.nl, 0900 0141; international calls 020 7940800*) is one of the busiest hub airports in the world and is also consistently voted one of its best. Myriad shops, bars, cafés, and restaurants are complemented by a mini branch of the Rijksmuseum, a spa, hotel, and casino. Located just 12 miles (20 km) south of Amsterdam, Schiphol is served by its own railroad station with direct services to Centraal Station every 15 minutes. Train tickets are available from the yellow ticket machines and in the ticket offices near the platforms at Schiphol Plaza. Direct journeys to Centraal Station take about 20 minutes and cost no more than €4.5 ($5) one-way *(National rail inquiries: www.ns.nl, 030 751 5155).*

Connexxion Schiphol Hotel Shuttle (*www.schipholhotelshuttle. nl, 088 339 4741*) vans travel frequently to and from Schiphol Plaza and virtually all hotels of the city. Tickets cost €29.5 ($33) round-trip.

Taxis are considerably more expensive than public transportation (approximately €40/$50), but worth considering if you're traveling in a group of four or more people. The official stand is just outside the main exit—it is strongly advised not to take rides from drivers soliciting within the airport. Allow 20 to 30 minutes from the airport to your hotel—more if you arrive in rush hour.

By Cruise Ship and Ferry
Increasing numbers of visitors arrive in Amsterdam by cruise ship, sailing right into the heart of the city to arrive at the striking **Passenger Terminal Amsterdam** (PTA; *www. ptamsterdam.nl, 020 509 1000*), with its wave-like, undulating roof. From here, it's a pleasant 15-minute walk along the waterside to Centraal Station. Alternatively, take Tram 26 from opposite the Muziekgebouw aan 't IJ (located just to the right of the PTA) or Tram 25, located to the left of the PTA.

A number of companies offer daily ferry services across the North Sea between England and the Netherlands. They include:
■ **DFDS Seaways** (*www.dfds. com; 330 333 0245*): Sails

daily from Newcastle to the Felison Terminal at the port of IJmuiden, on the outskirts of Amsterdam. From IJmuiden, it is a 35-minute drive to central Amsterdam by car or DFDS Seaways-operated bus service.
■ **P&O North Sea Ferries** (*www.poferries.com, 0130 444 8888*): A nightly service runs between Hull and Rotterdam's Europoort. It is a 90-minute drive from Rotterdam to Amsterdam. De Jong Tours operates a bus service from the Europoort to Rotterdam Centraal Station, and from here it is about one hour to Amsterdam Centraal Station (prebook tickets at the Reservations department).
■ **Stenaline** (*www.stenaline. nl, 0174 389 333*): Runs twice daily (day and overnight service) from Harwich to Hoek van Holland. It is an 80-minute drive from Hoek van Holland to Amsterdam or 1 hour 45 minutes by train (changing at Rotterdam), with regular departures from the port.

By Train
Fast, modern trains from all parts of Continental Europe arrive right in the heart of Amsterdam, at Centraal Station. There are several services a day from Paris, Brussels, Berlin, Cologne, Frankfurt, Luxembourg, and beyond (for details of international railroad services see the Dutch website, *www. nshispeed.nl*). From London, **Eurostar** provides a four-hour long train ride, or a seven-

hour passenger service to Amsterdam via Brussels (www. eurostar.com, 08432 186 186).

By Car

Each year, about a million tourists arrive in Amsterdam by car. At the hub of several trans-European highways, the city is easily reached by road from Continental Europe. However, the inner city is something of a maze, with very limited car parking. Drivers should make use of the parking garages and park & ride facilities located just outside of the central area. These offer excellent public transportation connections and many also incorporate bike rental in the cost of parking (www.iamsterdam.com). Drivers from the U.K. can bring their car using the ferry services (see p. 175) or the **Eurotunnel** shuttle service linking Folkestone to the French terminus at Calais (www. eurotunnel.com, UK: +44 08443 35 35 35; France: +33 0810 63 03 04).

GETTING AROUND AMSTERDAM

Public Transportation

Amsterdam has a fully integrated transportation system, incorporating trams, buses, Metro, and ferries, which link up to provide a seamless transition (en.gvb. nl). **OV-chipkaart** (PT Smart Card) tickets are valid for unlimited use on all forms of transportation. They can be supplemented with credit in euros. The **I amsterdam City Card** (available from Tourist Information and GVB ticket offices) also provides unlimited access to public transportation for 24, 48, 72, 96, or 120 hours. Most importantly, as you will be reminded while riding public transportation, don't forget to check in and check out on every journey you make. At the start of a journey, hold your card up to the reader until a green light appears. A bleeping sound will indicate that your card has been read. If you change to another bus/tram/Metro line, you have to check out (by scanning your card at the machine again) and check in again on your next bus/tram/Metro. If you forget to check out on any leg of your journey, the card will no longer be valid and you may risk a fine.

The hub of the city's public transportation system is Amsterdam **Centraal Station.** Buses and trams depart for all parts of the city from here. There is also a Metro station here and a ferry terminus (for free ferries to Amsterdam Noord). Near the Metro entrance (next to the I Amsterdam Visitor Centre) is a Service & Tickets kiosk of GVB, the authority that runs Amsterdam's public transportation, where you can buy tickets, travel cards, excursion packages, and route maps. Trams provide a comprehensive service within the city center, and are best suited to tourists, while buses are the best link to the suburbs, and the Metro is really intended for commuters, serving predominantly residential areas ringing the city.

Water

Trams will take you to your destination fast, but if you want a more leisurely ride, you can take to the water. Canal boat services provide a more romantic way of getting around, although they are not part of the public transportation system and are relatively expensive. Having said that, an **I amsterdam City Card** includes one free canal cruise and buying a ticket with the major cruise operators will give you discounted entry to a number of museums.

Stromma (www.stromma.com, 020 217 0500) and **Lovers** (www. lovers.nl, 020 530 1090) both offer 24-hour hop-on, hop-off tickets (Stromma also has a 48-hour option). These tickets give you discounts on admission to various museums.

Taxi

Traveling by taxi isn't generally necessary, unless you have lots of luggage or are running late. Regulations have been significantly tightened up recently, with the introduction of official, monitored taxi stands (you are not supposed to hail taxis in the street) and licensed cabs with regulated meters ensuring more consistent fares. Reserve a taxi through

Taxicentrale Amsterdam (TCA) by telephone or online *(www.tcataxi.nl, 020 777 7777)*. If time is not of the essence, consider calling a **Tuk Tuk** sightseeing taxi *(www.amsterdam-fietstaxi.nl, 06 5348 1860)* or bicycle taxi *(06 1859 5153)*.

Bicycle

Thanks to its compact size and extensive network of bike paths, Amsterdam is the perfect city to explore on two wheels, making bicycle rental an appealing option. However, for the uninitiated, the sheer numbers of cyclists on the roads, the labyrinth of bicycle paths, and coaster brakes take some getting used to. Before you hit the streets, familiarize yourself with your bike and the rules of the road.

MacBike *(www.macbike.nl, 020 624 83 91)* offers a free, multilingual leaflet on how to cycle safely through Amsterdam. Also be sure to follow instructions the vendor will give you on how to park and lock the bike in authorized locations, always securing it to a fixed, immovable object such as a lamppost. Failure to do so will incur the loss of your deposit, regardless of whether you have taken out insurance against the event of theft. To rent a bike, you will be asked to leave a blank credit card slip, or your passport/I.D. and a cash deposit. MacBike has a wide range of bicycles and outlets at Centraal Station, Leidseplein, Waterlooplein, and Marnixstraat.

PRACTICAL ADVICE

Currency

The Euro currency is used in the Netherlands: 100 euro cents make one euro. Coins are in denominations of 1c, 2c, 5c, 10c, 20c, 50c, €1, and €2. Notes are in €5, €10, €20, €50, €100, €200, and €500.

Credit cards are not used as widely as they are in most other European countries. They are still not accepted in major supermarkets or many smaller cafés, restaurants, or bars.

Electricity

Dutch sockets are of the Continental two-pin type, so you need a converter to use equipment with U.S. or U.K. plugs. The voltage (220, 50-cyle AC) is fine for U.K. equipment, but to use lower-voltage U.S. equipment you need a transformer.

Liquor & Narcotics

Individuals can legally buy and consume alcohol from the age of 18. Supermarkets and shops can only sell beer and wine or alcoholic beverages with an upper alcohol limit of 15 percent. Spirits are only sold in liquor stores.

Dutch law distinguishes between "soft drugs" (namely cannabis) and "hard drugs," allowing the personal use of the former by adults aged 18 and over in a limited, controlled way in designated coffeeshops. These coffeeshops are permitted to stock a maximum of 17.5 ounces (500 g) of cannabis at

any one time, and can sell a maximum of 0.17 ounce (5 g) to any adult. It is not legal to smoke cannabis anywhere outside of a designated coffeeshop.

The possession, use, and sale of hallucinogenic mushrooms (since 2008) and hard drugs (heroin, LSD, ecstasy, and cocaine) are illegal.

Media

You can buy the world's leading newspapers and magazines from the **Athenaeum Nieuwscentrum** *(Spui 14)*, **Waterstones** *(Kalverstraat 152)*, or the **American Book Center** *(Spui 12)*. The Dutch read *De Telegraaf* (establishment) and *De Volkskrant* (progressive). As you will hear if you take a taxi, most people listen to Radio 3, the commercial pop and chat channel (91.5 FM). More serious talk radio and news is broadcast (in Dutch) on Radio 5 (1008 AM).

Museum Card

If you intend to visit a number of museums while staying in Amsterdam, the **I amsterdam City Card** (see p. 176) gives access to some 40 attractions for 24, 48, 72, 96, or 120 hours. Alternatively, if you are visiting for a week or more and plan to visit other Dutch cities, consider purchasing a **Museumkaart** (Museum Card; *www.museumkaart.nl, 0900 4040 910*). Valid for a year, these cards cost €64.9 ($75) per adult and €32.45 ($35) for under 18s, and give unlimited access to some 400 museums across the

Netherlands, including the key attractions in Amsterdam.

Opening Hours

Shops are open from Monday to Saturday, 10 a.m. to 6 p.m. (Thursday evening until 9 p.m.), and Sunday, 12 p.m. to 5 p.m. Some supermarkets stay open until 8 p.m. or 10 p.m. on weeknights. Most businesses operate Monday to Friday, 8:30 a.m. to 5 p.m. Banks are open weekdays only, between 9 a.m. and 4 p.m.

Post Offices

Post offices are open weekdays only, between 9 a.m. and 5 p.m. However, Amsterdam's main post office, located in the basement of Singel 250 (020 620 3134), to the rear of the Royal Palace, has longer opening hours (8 a.m.–6 p.m. Mon.– Fri., 9 a.m.–5 p.m. on Sat., closed Sun.).

Public Holidays

Very little closes in Amsterdam except on the three big occasions of New Year's Day, King's Day (April 27 or April 26, if the 27th falls on a Sunday), and Christmas Day. In addition, the following are public holidays (some dates vary from year to year according to the liturgical calendar):
Easter Sunday and Monday (April or March)
Liberation Day (May 5)
Ascension Day (May or June)
Pentecost Monday and Sunday (May or June)
Sinterklaas (Dec. 5) Not an official public holiday, but many Dutch people take the day off.
Boxing Day (Dec. 26)

Restrooms

Men are reasonably well provided for in Amsterdam, with Parisian-style pissoirs located all around the city center. Streetside public conveniences are otherwise fairly rare. Traditionally people use café restrooms, but these are only for customers, so you should buy a drink before using the facilities. Museums and public buildings have clean, modern facilities, some of which might request a small tip for use, usually 20c or 50c.

Smoking

Smoking is officially banned in all bars, pubs, restaurants, and other public places.

Telephones

The city dialing code for Amsterdam is 020, which is not required when making calls within Amsterdam but only when you're outside the city. To make a local call from a public telephone in Amsterdam, you will need a telephone card, available from post offices, newsdealers, and several tourist offices. The international access code to call abroad from the Netherlands is 00, plus the code of the country you wish to call. When calling Amsterdam from abroad, dial 0031 (for the Netherlands) then 20 (for Amsterdam). In the Netherlands, toll phone numbers are preceded by the code 0800, premium rate lines by the code 0900, and mobile phones by 06.

Time Differences

The Netherlands observes Central European Time (CET),

one hour ahead of Greenwich Mean Time (GMT).

Tipping

Value added tax and service charges are included in hotel, restaurant, and shopping bills, and taxi fares. Tips for extra service are not necessary in cafés or bars unless you feel the service is outstanding. In restaurants, a tip of five to ten percent is always appreciated but not necessary: Pay the waiter directly by rounding up the bill. Tipping taxi drivers is rare, unless you get a particularly friendly one or receive assistance with luggage from him, in which case you can tip up to about ten percent of the fare.

Useful Phone Numbers

International directory inquiries: 1889
International and national operator: 0800 0410
National directory inquiries: 0900 8008

VISITOR INFORMATION

Tourist Information

Tourist information services are provided by the **VVV** (pronounced Fay Fay Fay in Dutch). There are branches dotted across the city, but the flagship office, called I Amsterdam Visitor Centre, is located in the cream-painted timber **Noord-Zuid Hollandsch Koffiehuis** building on the waterfront opposite Centraal Station (Stationsplein 10, 020 702 6000). It is open Mon.–Sat.

9 a.m.–6 p.m., and Sun. 10 a.m.–5 p.m. You can find another sizeable Tourist Offices at Schiphol Airport. You can book accommodations, excursions, boat trips, concert tickets, guided tours, and I amsterdam City Cards in person at these Tourist Offices or online (www.iamsterdam.com).

Useful Websites
www.dutchnews.nl
For Dutch news in English.
www.holland.com
The official tourism website of the Netherlands.
www.iamsterdam.com
A mine of information from the Tourist Office covering everything from the city's hotels and events to its history and last-minute deals and details of the I amsterdam City Card.
www.ns.nl
For national railway inquiries.
petitepassport.com/tag/ amsterdam/
An informative and entertaining blog by an Amsterdammer.
www.9292.nl
For public transportation advice.

EMERGENCIES

Police, Fire, & Ambulance
To summon any of these services, dial 112 from any telephone, free of charge. The emergency services operator will speak English. Tell them the address where the incident has taken place and the nearest landmark, crossroads, or house number, as well as where you are.

To report a theft to the police, or if you have other queries, dial 0900 8844. There are police stations in central Amsterdam (Nieuwezijds Voorburgwal 104 and Elandsgracht 117).

Embassies/Consulates
American Consulate
Museumplein 19, 020 575 5309
British Consulate
Koningslaan 44, 020 70 427 0427
Canadian Embassy Sophialaan 7, The Hague, 070 311 1600

Health Precautions
There are no inherent health risks involved in visiting Amsterdam. If you do need a doctor or dentist during your visit, ask your hotel reception for advice. If the problem is minor, go to the nearest pharmacy and speak to the pharmacist.
Ambulance, 112
Amsterdam tourist doctors, 020 237 3654
24-hour pharmacy information line, 020 592 3315 (Dutch-speaking, no guarantee of English, can advise on which outlets are nearest to you and open at the time of your call).

Public hospitals in Amsterdam that have 24-hour emergency departments include:
OLVG Hospital East
Eerste Oosterparkstraat 279, 020 599 9111

OLVG Hospital West Jan Tooropstraat 164, 020 510 8911

Lost or Stolen Credit Cards
Report any loss or theft immediately to your credit card company, so cards can be stopped, and to the local police station. Also phone your bank.

Lost Property
Always inform the police if you have lost something of value, to validate insurance claims. Report a lost passport to your embassy. Luggage lost on a train should be reported at the desk to the left of the luggage lockers in Centraal Station. For items lost in the city, contact the **Bureau Gevonden Voorwerpen** (Office of Lost Property; Korte Leidsestraat 52, + 31 14020).

Sensible Precautions
■ Keep valuables locked in the hotel safe.
■ Photocopy important documents and keep them separate.
■ Keep only a small amount of money with you.
■ Keep important documents and money in a closed bag when you carry them.
■ Do not leave your bag unattended at any time.
■ Do not travel alone at night, unless in a licensed taxi or along well-lit streets and in buses with other people.
■ Avoid parks at night.

HOTELS

TRAVEL ESSENTIALS

Amsterdam is one of Europe's most popular weekend destinations, with the small city barely having enough hotel rooms to meet the demand. For that reason, it is essential to reserve accommodations well in advance of your visit, not only to secure yourself a bed, but to avoid paying a premium for it. Amsterdam has experienced a much-needed hotel revolution in recent years, with new properties springing up across the city. Crucially, a disproportionately large number of these new additions are not large, chain hotels but chic, individually designed boutique hotels and bed and breakfasts.

In the throes of its exciting hotel revolution, Amsterdam offers unparalleled choice in accommodations, so it's well worth taking some time to consider your priorities when booking your base.

Given how compact the city is, location need not have too much bearing on your choice, although there is something magical about waking up to a view of ducks paddling down a tree-lined canal. Staying in an established hotel brings the benefits of a concierge, greater choice of amenities, and the ease of in-hotel dining, while a small bed and breakfast will offer more personalized service and an insight into local life.

Remaining true to the city's heritage and inimitable style, hotels like the **Canal House, JL No. 76,** and the **Conservatorium** have given historic buildings a new lease on life, dressing ancient sloping walls with modern art, placing rolltop baths by tall windows overlooking the canals, and commissioning handmade wallpaper based on traditional embroidered artworks.

By no means limited to making old look good,

Amsterdam's hip hotel scene also includes cutting-edge properties like **The Exchange,** which features rooms designed by students of the Amsterdam Fashion Institute (AMFI). The **Lloyd Hotel,** located in the Eastern Docklands, pioneered the concept of providing rooms ranging in quality (and price) from one to five star, while the **College Hotel** is staffed by students of the Amsterdam Hotel Management School. You can stay in a delightfully bijou bed and breakfast like the canalside **Kamer 01** in trendy de Pijp, blow the budget in the palatial, celebrity-studded **Hotel Amstel,** or spend the night on a houseboat or in a former water tower.

The **Amsterdam Visitor Centre** *(www.iamsterdam.com)* has access to an extensive directory that includes these properties and others across the city, and can advise on which might be best for you, if there is availability, and if there are any strong deals. This service is also available online.

Visitors with disabilities or particular needs in comfort, services, or anything else, should bear in mind that

smaller hotels located in historical buildings don't always have elevators or similar amenities, so check before you book.

Finally, don't rule out hotels in neighboring towns such as Den Haag, Rotterdam, Haarlem, Delft, and Utrecht. There are some charming properties in these atmospheric spots, which are invariably less expensive than Amsterdam and only a short train ride from the capital.

Price Range

An indication of the cost of a double room in the high season is given by € signs.

€€€€€ More than €300
€€€€ €220–€300
€€€ €150–€220
€€ €100–€150
€ Less than €100

Text Symbols

🛈 *No. of Guest Rooms*
🚌 *Public Transportation*
💳 *Credit Cards*

Organization

Hotels listed here have been grouped first according to neighborhood, then listed alphabetically by price range.

NIEUWE ZIJDE

Amsterdam's Nieuwe Zijde offers a number of elegant hotels in close proximity to Dam Square. Those that have rooms with canalside views are particularly worth seeking out.

■ GRAND HOTEL KRASNAPOLSKY
€€€€€
DAM 9, 1012 JS
TEL 020 554 9111
www.nh-hotels.com
A rather faded glory, the Krasnapolsky boasts a prime location on Dam Square, with fine views of the copper-domed Koninklijk Paleis and the central square. Besides its many rooms, the hotel has 35 furnished apartments, in restored historic houses, which are good for families.
🚪 451 🚋 *Tram: Dam*
💳 *All major cards*

■ HOTEL DE L'EUROPE
€€€€€
NIEUWE DOELENSTRAAT 2–14, 1012 CP
TEL 020 531 1777
www.leurope.nl
Built in the grand style of 1896, Hotel de l'Europe stands on the site of a medieval bastion at the junction of several canals and is almost entirely surrounded by water. The waterside setting can be enjoyed from spacious balconied rooms and the popular Marie brasserie. The gourmet Bord'eau Restaurant (one Michelin star) counts among Amsterdam's best, and Freddy's Bar (named after

former regular, Alfred "Freddy" Heineken) oozes atmosphere. The Junior Suites, decorated with replicas of many Dutch masterpieces, are particularly sought after.
🚪 111 🚋 *Tram: Muntplein*
💳 *All major cards*

■ DIE PORT VAN CLEVE
€€€€
NIEUWEZIJDS VOORBURGWAL 176–180, 1012 SJ
TEL 020 714 2000
www.dieportvancleve.nl
An Amsterdam stalwart, located by the Magna Plaza shopping center, Die Port van Cleve comprises three 18th-century houses and embraces Amsterdam's rich history, with lavish, traditional interiors. The blue-tiled Bar De Blauwe Parade serves traditional Dutch food: Sample authentic *erwtensoep* (split pea soup with ham hock) and delicious Zeeland mussels.
🚪 122 🚋 *Tram: Dam*
💳 *All major cards*

■ THE EXCHANGE
€€€€
DAMRAK 50, 1012 LL
TEL 020 523 0080
www.hoteltheexchange.com
The rooms of the innovative Exchange have been designed by students of the Amsterdam Fashion Institute (AMFI) in suitably quirky style. The "fashion hotel" allots rooms one- to five-star status, depending on their size, views, and amenities, but each is unique. A stone's throw from the Red-light District, it's at the heart of old Amsterdam

and popular with young visiting designers and fashionistas.
🚪 61 🚋 *Tram: Dam*
💳 *All major cards*

■ THE CRAFTSMEN
€€€
SINGEL 83, 1012 VE
TEL 020 210 1218
hotelthecraftsmen.com
This traditional little hotel offers fourteen rooms, each portraying a Dutch historical craft. The Craftsmen's location on the Singel means most rooms have canal views, and it's spitting distance from the medieval center's main sights. Two night minimum stay.
🚪 14 🚋 *Tram: Nieuwezijds Kolk*
💳 *All major cards*

OUDE ZIJDE

Many Oude Zijde hotels are housed in historic buildings that include 17th-century canal houses and one former palace. There are rooms to suit every taste—from traditional comfort to designer, boutique chic.

■ SOFITEL LEGEND AMSTERDAM THE GRAND
€€€€€
OUDEZIJDS VOORBURGWAL 197, 1012 EX
TEL 020 555 3111
www.sofitel.com
First a royal residence, then the City Hall, and later the Admiralty from where Holland's powerful navy was controlled, The Grand's magnificent rooms offer history as standard. More traditional than Amsterdam's

clutch of new hotels, The Grand is walking distance from popular sights and has a pretty garden and good spa.

ⓘ 177 🚋 *Tram: Dam*
🃏 *All major cards*

■ GRAND HOTEL AMRÂTH AMSTERDAM
€€€€
PRINS HENDRIKKADE 108, 1011 AK
TEL 020 552 0000
www.amrathamsterdam.com
The original art deco details of this former shipping house have been meticulously preserved, but the guest rooms are spacious, with a modern take on art nouveau style. Overlooking Oosterdok, with sweeping views of the city, the hotel celebrated its centenary in 2013, yet offers guests contemporary treats, including coffee machines, in each room and free entrance to its beautiful spa.

ⓘ 205 🚋 *Tram: Dam*
🃏 *All major cards*

■ MISC
€€€
KLOVENIERSBURGWAL 20, 1012 CV
TEL 020 330 6241
www.misceatdrinksleep.com
An excellent find in the Oude Zijde district, the boutique Misc features six guest rooms in a restored 17th-century canal house. Each looks out across the canal or a peaceful garden to the rear. Ranging from Design to Baroque, the rooms cater to all tastes, and the owners and their guests invariably end up chatting about their day in the inner courtyard garden.

Two night minimum stay (three nights in peak season).

ⓘ 6 🚋 *Tram: Centraal Station*
🃏 *All major cards*

JODENBUURT, PLANTAGE, & OOSTERDOK

These districts offer good-value rooms in innovative hotels, many of them within walking distance of the Eastern Docklands, Artis Royal Zoo, and Hortus Botanicus.

■ LLOYD HOTEL & CULTURAL EMBASSY
€€€–€€€€
OOSTELIJKE HANDELSKADE 34, 1019 BN
TEL 020 561 3636/020 561 3607
www.lloydhotel.com
Housed in a large, industrial-age building that has previously served as an immigrant hotel and a prison, the Lloyd Hotel is pioneering in many ways. Although everyone gets the same affable, efficient service, the guest rooms are rated from one to five star, guaranteeing that visitors of all budgets can benefit from its innovative design, popular restaurant, walking tours, and location in the Eastern Docklands district.

ⓘ 117 🚋 *Tram: Rietlandpark*
🃏 *All major cards*

■ HOTEL REMBRANDT
€€€
PLANTAGE MIDDENLAAN 17, 1018 DA
TEL 020 627 2714
www.hotelrembrandt.nl
Hotel Rembrandt is close

to Artis Royal Zoo and well located for the Tropenmusuem and Waterlooplein area. A small, quirky hotel, it has a curious breakfast room with mock medieval wall hangings, and some large and airy family rooms. Small doubles are tight but the largest rooms are at the front, where noise from trams might disturb light sleepers—ask for a back room overlooking the garden.

ⓘ 17 🚋 *Tram: Artis-Plantage Kerklaan* 🃏 *All major cards*

NORTHERN CANALS

This section of Amsterdam's impressive canal belt is good hunting ground for fun, independent hotels with fewer rooms and a personal touch.

■ ANDAZ AMSTERDAM
€€€€€
PRINSENGRACHT 587, 1016 HT
TEL 020 523 1234
www.hyatt.com
Quirky Amsterdam designer Marcel Wanders has created a hip, yet relaxed, sanctuary in the Andaz, a former public library on the Prinsengracht. Modern rooms feature decorative references to Amsterdam's history.

ⓘ 122 🚋 *Tram: Keizersgracht/ Prinsengracht* 🃏 *All major cards*

■ CANAL HOUSE
€€€€€
KEIZERSGRACHT 148, 1015 CX
TEL 020 622 5182
www.canalhouse.nl
This indulgent and seriously

sexy property with a delightful garden spreads across three historic canal houses. Guest rooms range in size and price from "good" to "exceptional," but all boast plush interiors, original artworks, and treats like rolltop baths and rain showers. Guests with a green thumb will enjoy the private garden. Rates include a generous buffet breakfast. Two night minimum stay.

(i) 23 ⮑ Tram: Westermarkt
◈ All major cards

■ HOTEL DE WINDKETEL
€€€€€
WATERTORENPLEIN 8C, 1051 PA
www.windketel.nl
This unusual property is located in Westerpark's car-free Eco-District. The Windketelgebouw ("air chamber building") is a small, three-story, octagonal turret that formed part of a handful of buildings built in the early 1900s. Local residents bought the tower and turned it into a mini "hotel," featuring a stylish kitchen, sitting room, and en-suite double bedroom surrounded by a small garden. Reservations can't be made for one-night stays. Animals and children under twelve are not allowed.

(i) 1 ⮑ Tram/Bus: Van Hallstraat
◈ No credit cards

■ THE TOREN
€€€
KEIZERSGRACHT 164, 1015 CZ
TEL 020 622 6033
www.toren.nl
Individual rooms in this classic boutique hotel vary from

bright and modern to exotic and intimate and include the Garden Cottage, which comes with its own in-room Jacuzzi. Enjoy an apéritif in the popular, wood-paneled bar before heading out for a stroll along the canals to dinner.

(i) 38 ⮑ Tram: Westermarkt
◈ All major cards

SOUTHERN CANALS

Hotels in the southern section of Amsterdam's canal belt include some of the city's grandest. Many have exceptional amenities and atmospheric canalside views.

■ AMSTEL INTERCONTINENTAL
€€€€€
PROFESSOR TULPPLEIN 1, 1018 GX
TEL 020 622 6060
www.amsterdam. intercontinental.com
The Amstel's slogan says it all: "The choice of Royalty, Nobility, and Celebrities since 1867." This prestigious hotel, set slightly apart from the bustle of Amsterdam on the Amstel River, prides itself on indulging its wealthy guests with attentive service, palatial rooms, romantic riverside views, and amazing food in its Restaurant La Rive. Two night minimum stay.

(i) 79 ⮑ Tram: Oosteinde
◈ All major cards

■ THE DYLAN HOTEL
€€€€€
KEIZERSGRACHT 384, 1016 GB
TEL 020 530 2010
www.dylanamsterdam.com
A tastefully and glamorously

decorated historic canalside property on the site of a 17th-century theater, which later became a Catholic almshouse and orphanage. Guest rooms feature original beams, ceilings, and fireplaces and are adorned with bold contemporary fabrics and high-tech amenities. A tranquil courtyard lies in the center of the hotel, the Michelin-starred restaurant Vinkeles is found in the ancient bakery, and the bar is popular for High Wine—wine flights accompanied by light Dutch bites. Two night minimum stay.

(i) 40 ⮑ Tram: Spui
◈ All major cards

■ KAMER 01
€€€€€
SINGEL 416, 1016 AK
TEL 06 5477 6151
www.kamer01.nl
Another classy bed and breakfast in a superb canalside location, with views of the flower market. The 16th-century house features a typically steep, narrow Amsterdam staircase, which brings you to three modern, stylish bedrooms—Red, Green, and Blue. Owners Peter and Wolter will treat you to a delicious organic breakfast, served either in your room or in the dining room. Two night minimum stay.

(i) 3 ⮑ Tram: Spui
◈ Visa, Mastercard

■ PULITZER
€€€€€
PRINSENGRACHT 323, 1016 GZ
TEL 020 523 5235
www.pulitzeramsterdam.com
The brainchild of art-loving

Peter Pulitzer, grandson of the newspaper publisher who founded the annual Pulitzer prizes, the Pulitzer Hotel comprises 25 restored 17th- and 18th-century canalside houses. The entire hotel is decorated with original artworks and antiques, and its gardens are delightful to stroll around and take afternoon tea in. Besides a good restaurant there is Pause at Pulitzer and Pulitzer's Bar, a fancy venue with leather lounges and classic drinks.

🛈 230 🚊 Tram: Westermarkt
💳 All major cards

■ SEVEN ONE SEVEN
€€€€€
PRINSENGRACHT 717, 1017 JW
TEL 020 427 0717
www.717hotel.nl
Number 717 Prinsengracht was once the home of a wealthy 19th-century sugar trader but, since 1997, it has been the site of an opulent, yet discrete hotel. Nine rooms and decadent suites are found here, with antique brass beds and marble floors. There's a cozy library and peaceful patio, where you can enjoy afternoon tea. Breakfast is served in your room, delivered in a wicker hamper.

🛈 11 🚊 Tram: Prinsengracht
💳 All major cards

■ MIAUW SUITES
€€€€
HARTENSTRAAT 34, 1016 CC
TEL 06 4603 6688
www.miauw.com
Located within two old houses and part of a complex incorporating pop-up design and fashion shops and studios, Miauw Suites are luxurious apartments in the heart of De Negen Straatjes. Each stylishly furnished suite features a bedroom, bathroom, living room (with a working desk and a 17-inch iMac computer), as well as all modern conveniences and toiletries.

🛈 3 🚊 Tram: Westermarkt
💳 All major cards

■ SEVEN BRIDGES HOTEL
€€
REGULIERSGRACHT 31, 1017 LK
TEL 020 623 1329
www.sevenbridgeshotel.nl
The name of this charming small hotel reflects its prime location at the point where the Reguliersgracht and Keizersgracht meet and from where you can see seven arched bridges. The property is an antique-lovers delight, with a 15th-century oak staircase, Louis XVI furniture, and baroque commodes mixing with Biedermeier and art deco pieces. There are no public rooms, so you can enjoy guilt-free continental breakfast in bed every day.

🛈 11 🚊 Tram: Rembrandtplein
💳 All major cards

MUSEUM DISTRICT & DE PIJP

Hotels in this area are ideal for high-end shopping and trips to a number of Amsterdam's finest museums. Many hotels here excel in combining maximum comfort with style.

■ COLLEGE HOTEL
€€€€€
ROELOF HARTSTRAAT 1, 1017 VE
TEL 020 571 1511
www.thecollegehotel.com
Located in a late 19th-century school building, College Hotel still plays an educational role—its staff are students of the Amsterdam Hotel Management School, overseen by a team of professionals from the Nedstede Hotel Group. Former classrooms are now sensuous, black-painted, and antique-littered guest rooms, the former gym houses an excellent restaurant, and locals go glamorous to sip cocktails in the sultry bar.

🛈 40 🚊 Tram: Roelof Hartplein
💳 All major cards

■ CONSERVATORIUM HOTEL
€€€€€
VAN BAERLESTRAAT 27, 1071 AN
TEL 020 570 0000
www.conservatorium hotel.com
Next door to the Stedelijk Museum, adjacent to the Concertgebouw, and a stone's throw from the Rijksmuseum, the Conservatorium occupies one of the best locations of any hotel in this city. Originally built as a bank, then taken over by Amsterdam University's Sweelinck Conservatorium of Music, it received a makeover from Italian architect and interior designer Piero Lissoni. Cutting-edge design combines with

imaginative elements like the trees planted in the basement, whose tips emerge at ground level by the bar. The result is slick, buzzing, and justifiably popular. Don't miss the fine dining options and the amazing spa.

ⓘ 129 🚊 *Tram: Van Baerlestraat*
🔷 *All major cards*

■ JL NO. 76
€€€€
JAN LUIJKENSTRAAT 76, 1071 CT
TEL 020 348 5555/020 515 0453
www.hoteljlno76.com
Located down the road from the Rijksmuseum and around the corner from the popular P. C. Hooftstraat and Cornelis Schuytstraat shopping streets, this is an understated, urban-chic hotel. The hospitable owner, Arjen van den Hof, invites guests to enjoy his art collection, use the honesty bar, and pick his brains for local tips. Two night minimum stay, pets not allowed.

ⓘ 39 🚊 *Tram: Van Baerlestraat*
🔷 *All major cards*

■ OKURA
€€€€
FERDINAND BOLSTRAAT 333, 1072 LH
TEL 020 678 7111
www.okura.nl
Given its size, proximity to Schiphol airport and the RAI Conference Center, and four excellent restaurants (including two Japanese establishments, one of which is a Michelin-starred restaurant), Okura is popular with business travelers. Guest rooms are well-appointed but not as individual as rooms in many of Amsterdam's smaller hotels. The top-floor Ciel Bleu restaurant, one of Amsterdam's Michelin-starred restaurants, and the trendy Twenty Third Bar offer mesmerizing views across the city.

ⓘ 300 🚊 *Tram: Cornelis Troostplein/ Scheldestraat*
🔷 *All major cards*

■ HOTEL ARENA
€€€
'S-GRAVESANDESTRAAT 55, 1092 AA
The entrance to the Hotel Arena is inside the Oosterpark. The nature that surrounds the hotel makes it very serene, despite being located near the city center (which you can reach in under 10 minutes with one of the bicycles available for rent from the hotel). Situated in a renovated ex-orphanage, the building has maintained many of its original decorations and structures.

🚊 *Tram: Alexanderplein*
🔷 *All major cards*

INDEX

Page numbers in *italic* refer to map pages

A
afternoon tea 27
air travel 175
Albert Cuypmarkt 105, *149*, 156
Allard Pierson Museum *67*, 75
American Hotel *21*, 23, 168
Amstel Hotel *24*, 27
Amsterdam Central Library *33*, 34, 171
Amsterdam Gallery 17
Amsterdam merchant ship 95
Amsterdam Museum *14*, 17, *28*, 30, *47*, 56–59
Amsterdam School architectural movement 48–49, 115–116
Andersson, Sven-Ingvar 150
Andriessen, Mari 23
Anne Frank House *14*, 17, *18*, 22, *109*, 118–121
Anne Frank (statue) 23, 111
apple pie 124
architecture
    Amsterdam School 48–49, 115–116
    Dutch classical style 52, 77
    Gothic 48, 51, 71
    modernist 48–49
    neo-Renaissance 48, 151
    neoclassical 92, 137
    roof gables 135
    Viennese classicism 151–152
    see also art deco & art nouveau
art & antiques district *130*, 136
art deco & art nouveau
    1e Klas café-restaurant 62
    Bistro Berlage 49
    Café Americain *21*, 168
    The Movies 114
    Sauna Deco 170
    Zuiderbad 23, *37*, 39, 168
art market 102
Artis Royal Zoo *33*, 34, *87*, 93–94
Artplein Spui 102

B
ballet 22, 82–83
banks 178

beer & breweries 122–123, *149*, 156–157, 171
Begijnhof 17, *47*, 53–54
Berlage, H. P. 49, 151
Beurs van Berlage *46*, 48–49
Bickerseiland 114
bike rental 9, 61, 177
Biologische Versmarkt 104–105
Blauwe Theehuis 23, 154–155
Bloemen en Plantenmarkt 103
Bloemenmarkt *47*, 55, 102–103
Bloemgracht 17
Boerenmarkt 104
book market 53, 103–104
Breitner, George Hendrik 114
brown cafés 81

C
cabaret 83
Café Americain *21*, 168
Café In 't Aepjen 68
Campen, Jacon van 52
canal boat trips 23, *36*, 38
canal bus 16, 23, 132, 145, 176
Canal Festival 145
Canal Ring 8, 144
canals 16, 144–145
cannabis 80–81, 177
Cat Boat 62–63
Cat Museum *130*, 137–138
Centraal Station *46*, 48, 62, 176
cheeses 126
children's Amsterdam 32–37
Children's Farm 117
Children's Museum 89
Chinatown 68
churches
    English Reformed Church 17, 54
    Nieuwe Kerk 17, *28*, 30, *46*, 51
    Oude Kerk *66*, 71–72
    Posthoornkerk 113–114
    "Secret Chapel" 54
    Sint Nicolaaskerk *28*
    Southern Church *67*, 74
    Westerkerk 22–23, *109*, 111
    Western Church 22–23, *109*, 111
    Zuiderkerk *67*, 74
cinema 116
    EYE Film Institute Netherlands 16, *37*, 39
    The Movies 114

Theater Pathé Tuschinski 169
climate 174–175
Coalition Project 1012 70, 78
CoBrA art movement 17, 160
coffeeshops 80–81, 177
concert venues 51, 83, 151–153
Concertgebouw 83, *148*, 151–153
credit cards 177, 179
cruise ships 175
currency 177
Cuypers, P. J. H. 48, 113, 150, 151–152
cycling 60–61, 177
    bike rental 9, 61, 177
    safety 60, 177
    tours 61

D
Dam Square *14*, 17, *18*, *28*, 30, *46*, 50–51
Damrak 45, 50
De Bijenkorf department store 51
De Brakke Grond arts center 82
De Negen Straatjes *18*, 22, *25*, 26, *130*, 138–139
De Prael 171
De Schreierstoren *28*, 30, *67*, 72
De Waag *28*, 31, *66*, 68–69
De Wallen *see* Red-light District
dentists 179
design emporiums 166–167
diamond works *25*, 26
discounts 9, 176, 177–178
doctors 179
dollhouse collection 160
doll's hospital 139
Drag Queen Olympics 111
driving 176
Droog 166
drugs 80–81, 177
Dutch East India Company 31, 90
Dutch National Opera & Ballet 22, 82–83
Dutch West India Company 30

E
electricity 177
Elegantiersgracht 144
embassies & consulates 179
emergencies 179

INDEX

English Reformed Church 17, 54
entrance fees 11
Erotic Museum 70
EYE Film Institute Netherlands 16, *37*, 39

F
farmer's market 104
fast-food outlets 125
ferry services 175
festivals 174
flea markets *19*, *86*, 88, 102
flower market *47*, *55*, 102–103
Fo Guang Shan Buddhist Temple 68
Foam Museum *131*, 135
food & drink
  afternoon tea 27
  beer & breweries 122–123, *149*, 156–157, 171
  Dutch cuisine 124–127
  jenever 122–123
  liquor laws 177
  picnicking 17, 38, 150
  price ranges 11
Frank, Anne 111
  see also Anne Frank House
Frozen Fountain 167

G
gardens and parks
  Hortus Botanicus *32*, 35, *87*, 90–91
  Keukenhof Park 143
  Leidsebosje 62
  Open Garden Days 141
  Vondelpark *20*, *36*, 38, *149*, 154–155
  Westergasfabriek Culture Park *108*, 116–117
Gassan Diamonds *25*, 26
gay community 110–111
Geldersekade 144
Gendt, Adolf van 151–152
Golden Bend 137, 144
Gouden Bocht 137, 144
Gouden Reael 114–115
Grachtengordel 8, 144
graffiti 62
Great Synagogue 88–89

Groenburgwal 144
guilds 31, 68–69
Gustafson, Kathryn 117

H
Haarlemerstraat *109*, 113–114
Haarlemmerpoort 114
Halverstad, Raphaël 100, 101
Hash, Marihuana, & Hemp Museum 81
health 179
Heineken Experience *149*, 156–157
HEMA retail chain 167
Hepburn, Audrey 152
Herengracht 135, 137, 144
Hermitage Amsterdam *131*, 132–134, 168–169
herring 127
Het Houten Huys 54
"Het Kleine Weeshuis" 58
Het Lieverdje (The Little Darling) 53
Het Scheepvaartmuseum *86*, 94–95
hofjes 113
Hollandsche Manege 23, *36*, 38
Hollandsche Schouwburg *87*, 91–92, 100
Homomonument 23, *109*, 110–111
Hortus Botanicus *32*, 35, *87*, 90–91
hotels 180–185
Houseboat Museum *130*, 139
Hudson, Henry 30, 72
hutspot (hotchpotch) 125

I
I amsterdam City Card 9, 176, 177
ice-skating 150
Indonesian cuisine 125
inline skating 38
insurance 175

J
Jacob Hooy & Co. 66, 69–70
jenever 122–123
Jewish community 88–89, 91–92, 98–101, 118–121

Jodenbuurt, Plantage, & Oosterdok 84–105, *106–107*
  Artis Royal Zoo 33, 34, *87*, 93–94
  Children's Museum 89
  Great Synagogue 88–89
  Het Scheepvaartmuseum *86*, 94–95
  Hollandsche Schouwburg *87*, 91–92, 100
  Hortus Botanicus *32*, 35, *87*, 90–91
  hotels 182
  Joods Historisch Museum *87*, 88–89
  Museum het Rembrandthuis *19*, *29*, 31, *86*, 96–97
  National Maritime Museum *86*, 94–95
  New Synagogue 89
  Portuguese Synagogue 89
  Resistance Museum *29*, 31, *87*, 92–93
  Verzetsmuseum *29*, 31, *87*, 92–93
  Waterloopleinmarkt *19*, 22, *86*, 88, 102
Joods Historisch Museum *87*, 88–89
Jordaan 17, *109*, 112–113

K
Kattenkabinet *130*, 137–138
Keizersgracht 135, 145
Kerkstraat 135
Ketelhuis 116
Keukenhof Park 143
Keyser, Hendrick de 55, 73, 74, 111
King's Day 38, 110, 174, 178
Klerk, Michel de 115
Koninklijk Paleis 17, 28, 30, *47*, 52–53

L
Lapjesmarkt 104
Leidsebosje 62
Leidsegracht 144
libraries
  airport library 63

INDEX

Amsterdam Central Library *33, 34,* 171
licorice 125
Lijnbaansgracht 135
liquor laws 177
"The Little Orphanage" 58
live-music venues
    Paradiso *24, 27*
    see also concert venues; opera
lost property 179

M
Madame Tussauds 51
Magere Brug *131,* 132, 145
markets 102–105
    Albert Cuypmarkt 105, *149,* 156
    art market 102
    Artplein Spui 102
    Biologische Versmarkt 104–105
    Bloemen-en-Plantenmarkt 103
    Bloemenmarkt *47,* 55, 102–103
    Boerenmarkt 104
    book market 53, 103–104
    flea markets 19, *86,* 88, 102
    flower market *47,* 55, 102–103
    Lapjesmarkt 104
    Noordermarkt 104
    organic markets 104–105
    Waterlooppleinmarkt 19, 22, *86,* 88, 102
meatballs 126
medical services 179
Melkweg 83
Meulendijks & Schuil 136
Miracle of Amsterdam 54
Mirror Quarter *130,* 136
Mondriaan, Piet 17
Monet, Claude 74
money 177
Montelbaanstoren *67,* 73, 97
Moooi 167
Movies, The 114
Munttoren *47,* 54–55
Museum District & de Pijp 146–171, *148–149*
    Albert Cuypmarkt 105, *149,* 156
    Concertgebouw 83, *148,* 151–153
    Heineken Experience *149,* 156–157
    hotels 184–185

Museumplein *148,* 150
P. C. Hooftstraat *24, 27, 149,* 153–154
Rijksmuseum *15,* 16–17, *20, 23, 148,* 158–161
Stedelijk Museum *20, 148,* 150–151
Van Gogh Museum *21, 37,* 39, *148,* 162–165
Vondelpark *20, 36,* 38, *149,* 154–155
Museum het Rembrandthuis *19, 29,* 31, *86,* 96–97
Museum het Schip *108,* 115–116
Museum van Loon *130,* 140–141
Museum Willet-Holthuysen *131,* 134
Museumkaart 177–178
Museumplein *148,* 150
museums & galleries
    Allard Pierson Museum *67,* 75
    Amsterdam Gallery 17
    Amsterdam Museum 14, 17, *28,* 30, *47,* 56–59
    Anne Frank House 14, 17, *18,* 22, *109,* 118–121
    Cat Museum *130,* 137–138
    Children's Museum 89
    Erotic Museum 70
    EYE Film Institute Netherlands 16, *37,* 39
    Foam Museum *131,* 135
    Hash, Marihuana, & Hemp Museum 81
    Hermitage Amsterdam *131,* 132–134, 168–169
    Het Scheepvaartmuseum *86,* 94–95
    Hollandsche Schouwburg *87,* 91–92
    Houseboat Museum *130,* 139
    Joods Historisch Museum *87,* 88–89
    Kattenkabinet *130,* 137–138
    Museum het Rembrandthuis *19, 29,* 31, *86,* 96–97
    Museum het Schip *108,* 115–116
    Museum van Loon *130,* 140–141
    Museum Willet-Holthuysen *131,* 134

National Maritime Museum *86,* 94–95
NEMO *33,* 34
Our Lord in the Attic *66,* 76–77
Resistance Museum *29,* 31, *87,* 92–93
Rijksmuseum *15,* 16–17, *20, 23, 148,* 158–161
Stedelijk Museum *20, 148,* 150–151
Tropenmuseum *32,* 35
Van Gogh Museum *21, 37,* 39, *148,* 162–165
Verzetsmuseum *29,* 31, *87,* 92–93
Woonbootmuseum *130,* 139

N
Nationaal Monument 50
National Maritime Museum *86,* 94–95
Nazi Occupation 31, 92–93, 98–101
NDSM-werf *15,* 16
Neerlandia Building 134
neighborhood walks 11, *42–43*
    Jodenbuurt, Plantage, & Oosterdok 84–105, *86–87*
    Museum District & de Pijp 146–171, *148–149*
    Nieuwe Zijde 44–63, *46–47*
    northern canals 106–127, *108–109*
    Oude Zijde 64–83, *66–67*
    southern canals 128–145, *130–131*
NEMO *33,* 34
Nes 82
New Synagogue 89
newspapers and magazines 177
Nieuwe Kerk 17, *28,* 30, *46,* 51
Nieuwe Zijde 44–63, *46–47*
    Amsterdam Museum 14, 17, *28,* 30, *47,* 56–59
    Begijnhof 17, *47,* 53–54
    Beurs van Berlage *46,* 48–49
    Bloemenmarkt *47,* 55, 102–103
    Centraal Station *46,* 48, 62, 176
    Dam Square 14, 17, *18, 28,* 30, *46,* 50–51
    English Reformed Church 17, 54

INDEX

flower market *47, 55*, 102–103
Het Houten Huys (Wooden
  House) 54
hotels 181
Koninklijk Paleis *17, 28, 30, 47,*
  52–53
Madame Tussauds 51
Munttoren *47,* 54–55
Nationaal Monument 50
Nieuwe Kerk *17, 28, 30, 46,* 51
"Secret Chapel" 54
Nieuwmarkt *17,* 68
Nine Streets *18, 22, 25, 26, 130,*
  138–139
Noordermarkt 104
northern canals 106–127,
  108–109
  Anne Frank House *14, 17, 18,*
    22, 109, 118–121
  Haarlemerstraat *109,* 113–114
  Haarlemmerpoort 114
  Homomonument *23, 109,*
    110–111
  hotels 182–183
  Jordaan *17, 109,* 112–113
  Museum het Schip *108,*
    115–116
  Posthoornkerk 113–114
  Westelijk Eilanden *108,* 114–115
  Westergasfabriek Culture Park
    108, 116–117
  Westerkerk 22–23, *109,* 111
  Western Church 22–23, *109,*
    111
  Western Islands *108,* 114–115

O
oliebollen (deep-fried doughnuts)
  127
Oost-Indisch Huis *29,* 31
Oosterdok *see* Jodenbuurt,
  Plantage, *&* Oosterdok
Open Garden Days 141
open-air concerts 38
open-air theater 23, 38, 155
open-year-round attractions 8
Openbare Bibliotheek Amsterdam (OBA) *33, 34,* 171
opening hours 178
opera 22, 82–83
organic markets 104–105

orientation 8, 9
Oud-Zuid district 27
Oude Kerk *66,* 71–72
Oude Zijde 64–83, *66–67*
  Allard Pierson Museum *67,* 75
  Chinatown 68
  De Schreierstoren *67,* 72
  De Waag *28,* 31, *66,* 68–69
  Erotic Museum 70
  Fo Guang Shan Buddhist
    Temple 68
  hotels 181–182
  Jacob Hooy *&* Co. *66,* 69–70
  Montelbaanstoren *67,* 73, 97
  Oude Kerk *66,* 71–72
  Our Lord in the Attic *66,* 76–77
  Red-light District *14,* 17, *18, 66,*
    70, 78–79
  Zeedijk *66,* 68
  Zuiderkerk *67,* 74
Oudemanhuispoort Book Market
  53, 103–104
Oudeschans 73
Oudezijds Achterburgwal 70
Oudezijds Kolk 68
Oudezijds Voorburgwal 144
Our Lord in the Attic *66,* 76–77

P
pancakes 124
Paradiso 24, 27
passports 175
P. C. Hooftstraat *24, 27, 149,*
  153–154
pea soup 125
Peek *&* Cloppenburg
  department store 51
performing arts 82–83
Peter Stuyvesant (statue) 30
pharmacies 179
Piano, Renzo 34
Picasso, Pablo 23
picnicking 17, 38, 150
Pijp *see* Museum District *&*
  de Pijp
Pimentel, Henriëtte 100, 101
Planetarium 94
Plantage *see* Jodenbuurt, Plantage, *&* Oosterdok
playground 34, 171
Poezenboot 62–63

police 179
pony camps 38
Portuguese Synagogue 89
post offices 178
Posthoornkerk 113–114
Prinseneiland 114
Prinsengracht 17, 135, 145
proeflokalen (tasting rooms)
  123, 171
prostitution 78–79
  see also Red-light District
public holidays 178
public transportation 176–177

Q
Quellinus, Artus 53

R
radio 177
rainy-day activities 168–171
Realeneiland 114
Red-light District *14,* 17, *18, 66,*
  70, 78–79
Reguliersgracht *131,* 135, 144
Rembrandt 22, 31, 71, 73, 111
  "The Night Watch" 160–161
  see also Museum het
    Rembrandthuis
Resistance Museum *29,* 31, *87,*
  92–93
restrooms 178
riding school 23, *36,* 38
Rietveld, Gerrit 162
Rijksmuseum *15,* 16–17, *20,* 23,
  148, 158–161
roof gables 135
Royal Tropical Institute 35
Ruisdael, Jacob van 73, 77

S
safety
  cycling 60, 177
  sensible precautions 179
St. Anthony Sluice 97
Sauna Deco 170
Schiphol Airport 63, 175
seasons 174–175
secret Amsterdam 62–63
"Secret Chapel" 54
Seven Bridges 135, 144

sex trade 78–79
see also Red-light District
shopping
  design emporiums 166–167
  opening hours 178
  tour 24–27
  vintage shopping 102, 104, 139
  see also markets
Sint Antoniesluis 97
Sint Nicolaaskerk 28
Skinny Bridge 131, 132, 145
smoking 178
southern canals 128–145, 130–131
  Cat Museum 130, 137–138
  De Negen Straatjes 18, 22, 25,
    26, 130, 138–139
  Foam Museum 131, 135
  Hermitage Amsterdam 131,
    132–134, 168–169
  hotels 183–184
  Houseboat Museum 130, 139
  Kattenkabinet 130, 137–138
  Magere Brug 131, 132, 145
  Mirror Quarter 130, 136
  Museum van Loon 130,
    140–141
  Museum Willet-Holthuysen
    131, 134
  Nine Streets 18, 22, 25, 26, 130,
    138–139
  Reguliersgracht 131, 135, 144
  Skinny Bridge 131, 132, 145
  Spiegelkwartier 130, 136
  Woonbootmuseum 130, 139
Southern Church 67, 74
Spiegelkwartier 130, 136
Spui 53, 102
Stadsschouwburg 83
statues and memorials
  Anne Frank 23, 111
  Het Lieverdje (The Little
    Darling) 53
  Homomonument 23, 109,
    110–111
  Nationaal Monument 50
  Peter Stuyvesant 30

Wall of Remembrance 92
Stedelijk Museum 20, 148,
  150–151
street art 62
stroopwafels (cookies) 126–127
Stuyvesant, Peter 30
Süskind, Walter 100–101
swimming pool 23, 37, 168

T
taxis 176–177
telephones 178
"The Night Watch" (Rembrandt)
  160, 161
theater 23, 38, 82, 83, 155
Theater Tuschinski 169
theft 179
time differences 178
tipping 178
toilets 178
tourist information 178–179
tours
  Concertgebouw 153
  cycling 61
  Heineken Experience 156–157
  Red-light District 79
train services 175–176
trams 176
traveling around Amsterdam
  176–177
traveling to Amsterdam 175–176
Trompettersteeg 70
Tropenmuseum 32, 35
tulips 142–143
TunFun Speelpark 34, 171

U
Utrechtsestraat 25, 26

V
Van Brienenhofje 113
Van Gogh Museum 21, 37, 39,
  148, 162–165
Verzetsmuseum 29, 31, 87, 92–93
views of Amsterdam 49, 111, 144
vintage shopping 102, 104, 139

Vondelpark 20, 36, 38, 149,
  154–155

W
Wall of Remembrance 92
Waterloopleinmarkt 19, 22, 86,
  88, 102
websites 179
Weissman, Adriaan Willem 151
West-Indisch Huis 28, 30, 113
Westelijk Eilanden 108, 114–115
Westergasfabriek Culture Park
  108, 116–117
Westerkerk 22–23, 109, 111
Western Church 22–23, 109, 111
Western Islands 108, 114–115
when to go 174
whirlwind tours 10
  Amsterdam for History Lovers
    28–31
  Amsterdam for Shoppers
    24–27
  Amsterdam in a Day 14–17
  Amsterdam in a Weekend
    18–23
  Amsterdam in a Weekend with
    Kids 32–39
Wooden House 54
Woonbootmuseum 130, 139
World War II 31, 50, 89, 91–93,
  98–101, 110, 118–121
Wren, Christopher 74

Z
Zeedijk 66, 68
Zon's Hofje 113
zoo 33, 34, 87, 93–94
Zuiderbad 37, 39, 168
Zuiderkerk 67, 74

CREDITS

Author
Pip Farquharson

Additional text by Reg Grant, Tony Halliday, Alice Peebles, Joe Yogerst

Picture credits
Abbreviations: GI (Getty Images), SH (Shutterstock .com), SS (SuperStock) t = top, b = bottom, l = left, r = right, m = middle.

2–3 F1 online digitale Bildagentur GmbH/Alamy; **4** Yadid Levy/ National Geographic; **5tr, mr** National Geographic; **5bl** Tony Halliday; **6** Yadid Levy/National Geographic; **9** devy/SH; **12–13** George Tsafos/Lonely Planet Images/GI; **14t** Gertan/SH; **14b** BESTWEB/SH; **15t** Aija Lehtonen/SH; **15b** Yadid Levy/ National Geographic; **16** Yadid Levy/National Geographic; **18t** Yadid Levy/National Geographic; **18b** Colin Dutton/ SIME/4Corners Images; **19t** Yadid Levy/National Geographic; **19b** Ivonne Wierink/SH; **20t** John Lewis Marshall; **20mr** Yadid Levy/National Geographic; **20bl** pentothal/SH; **21** Yadid Levy/National Geographic; **23** Mikhail Markovskiy/SH; **24t** Shawn Chin; **24m** Volodymyr Krasyuk/SH; **24b** devy/SH; **25t** Goldsmith Gassan Diamonds; **25b** Laura Balvers/Shutterstock; **26** Yadid Levy/National Geographic; **28r** imagebroker. net/SS; **28l** Oleg Senkov/SH; **29t** Tony Halliday; **29b** Gert Jan van Rooy/Dutch Resistance Museum **30** TonyV3112/SH; **32t** De Hortus Amsterdam; **32b** Tropenmuseum; **33t** Ton Koene/ age fotostock/SS; **33b** r.martens/ SH; **35** Tropenmuseum; **36t** Magnus Ragnvid/GI; **36m** Hollandsche Manege; **36b** AA

World Travel Library/Alamy; **37t** Igor Plotnikov/SH; **37b** Tony Halliday; **39** Yadid Levy/ National Geographic; **40–41** Yadid Levy/National Geographic; **44** National Geographic; **46** jorisvo/SH; **47l** Menna/SH; **47r** Tony Halliday; **49** Tony Halliday; **50** Tony Halliday; **51** Yadid Levy/ National Geographic; **52** Yadid Levy/National Geographic; **53** Mikel Bilbao/age fotostock/ SH; **54** Tony Halliday; **55** Yadid Levy/National Geographic/ SS; **56** Netherlands Board of Tourism & Conventions; **57** Ken Walsh/Alamy; **59** Yadid Levy/ National Geographic; **60** Tony Halliday **61** Roman Sigaev/SH; **63** imagebroker.net/SS; **64** Yadid Levy/National Geographic; **66t** Tony Halliday; **66b** National Geographic; **67** Yadid Levy/ National Geographic; **69** imagebroker.net/SS; **71** lynnlin/ SH; **73** Tony Halliday; **74–75** Prisma/SH;**76** Aldo Pavan/ SIME/4Corners; **78** Marka/SS; **79** Tony Halliday; **80–81** Tony Halliday; **82** devy/SH; **84** Tony Halliday; **86l** Yadid Levy/National Geographic; **86r** Tony Halliday; **87** Tony Halliday; **89** Yadid Levy/ National Geographic; **90** Yadid Levy/National Geographic; **93** r.martens/SH; **95** Yadid Levy/ National Geographic; **96** Yadid Levy/National Geographic; **99** Ullstein bild/TopFoto; **100** Tony Halliday; **101**Hemis.fr/SS; **103** Jean Pierre Lescourret/Lonely Planet Images/GI; **104** graja/SH; **105** Hemis.fr/SS; **106** Stefano Amantini/4Corners; **108** Yadid Levy/National Geographic; **109** Mario Savoia/SH; **110** Lonely Planet Images/GI; **112** National Geographic; **114–115** Yadid Levy/National Geographic; **116** imagebroker.net/SS; **117** Ton Koene/age fotostock/

SS; **118–121** Anne Frank Fonds – Basel/Anne Frank House/ GI; **122** Martin Child/GI; **123** Hemis.fr/SS; **124** Tony Halliday; **126** Yadid Levy/National Geographic; **127** Tony Halliday; **128** National Geographic; **130** Yadid Levy/National Geographic; **131t** Tony Halliday; **131b** Yadid Levy/National Geographic; **132** Smelov/Shutterstock **133–136** Yadid Levy/National Geographic; **137** Kattenkabinet Amsterdam; **138** Yadid Levy/ National Geographic; **140** Tony Halliday; **142** Mario Savoia/ SH; **143** Gertan/SH; **145** Yadid Levy/National Geographic; **147** Michael Kooren/Reuters/ Corbis; **148** Lonely Planet Images/Getty; **149** ©Heinken Brouwerijen B.V., Amsterdam; **150** Tony V3112/SH; **151** Sol LeWitt, Wall Drawing #1084, 2003-2012. Collection Stedelijk Museum Amsterdam; **152** Concertgebouw **155** National Geographic; **156** Ppictures/ SH; **157** ©Heinken Brouwerijen B.V.,Amsterdam; **158** Ton Koene/ dpa/Corbis; **161–162** Yadid Levy/National Geographic; **165** Fine Art Images/SS; **166** courtesy of Droog; **167** Colin Dutton/SIME/4Corners; **169** imagebroker.net/SS; **170** Tony Halliday; **172–173** Jean-Pierre Lescourret.

Since 1888, the National Geographic Society has funded more than 14,000 research, exploration,
and preservation projects around the world. National Geographic Partners distributes a portion of the funds it receives from your purchase
to National Geographic Society to support programs including the conservation of animals and their habitats.

National Geographic Partners, LLC
1145 17th Street NW
Washington, DC 20036-4688 USA

Get closer to National Geographic explorers and photographers, and connect with our global community. Join us today at
nationalgeographic.com/join

For rights or permissions inquiries, please contact National Geographic Books Subsidiary Rights: bookrights@natgeo.com

Copyright © 2014, 2021 National Geographic Partners, LLC. All rights reserved. Reproduction of the whole
or any part of the contents without written permission from National Geographic Partners, LLC is prohibited.

NATIONAL GEOGRAPHIC and Yellow Border Design are trademarks of the National Geographic Society, used under license.

Edition edited by White Star s.r.l.
Licensee of National Geographic Partners, LLC.
Update by Iceigeo, Milan (Camilla Pelizzoli, Cynthia Anne Koeppe, Alberto Brambilla, Maria-Angela Silleni)

The information in this book has been carefully checked and to the best of our knowledge is accurate. However, details are subject
to change, and the publisher cannot be responsible for such changes, or for errors or omissions. Assessments of sites, hotels, and
restaurants are based on the author's subjective opinions, which do not necessarily reflect the publisher's opinion.

Printed by
Rotolito S.p.A. - Seggiano di Pioltello (MI) - Italy

192 | WALKING AMSTERDAM